REINVENTING TEXTILES

REINVENTING TEXTILES

Volume 1
Tradition and Innovation

Edited by Sue Rowley

TELOS

© Sue Rowley, 1999
Edited by Sue Rowley
Series Coordinator: Matthew Koumis
Proof reader: Katherine James
Cover design by KR, Italy
Printed by La Commerciale Borgogno, Italy

ISBN 1 902015 002

A CIP catalogue record for this book is available from the British Library

First published in 1999 with support from Southern Arts
Reprinted with corrections in Italy, 2004

Telos Art Publishing
1 Highland Square
Clifton, Bristol
BS8 2YB, England
T/F +44 (0)117 923 9124
editorial@telos.net
www.arttextiles.com

Photo credits
p. 2 Barry Allwright
p. 22 Jan Ross Manley
p. 35, plate 2 Jasleen Dhamija
p. 48, plate 4, plate 5 courtesy of Bradford Art Galleries and Museums
p. 69, plate 13 London Printworks
p. 92, plate 10, plate 11 Lech Andrzejewski
p. 96 B Sanchez
p. 107 A Lopez
plate 1 Maningrida Arts and Culture
plate 3 Lynn Setterington
plate 8 Michael Young
pp. 78, 115, 141, plates 6a, 6b,14, 15,16 courtesy of the artist

ISBN 1-9020150-0-2

9 781902 015002

ACKNOWLEDGEMENTS

The Editor wishes to thank the contributors for the esssays, and the artists whose work is reproduced here. The readership for a book of essays about textile art is indeterminate and I thank Telos Art Publishing for its publication. Matthew Koumis has been more patient than I could reasonably have expected, and I thank him very much for seeing the book through to completion. Diana Wood Conroy has been a 'travelling companion' and friend and she will recognise several ideas here which have been developed with her in conversation. In editing this collection of essays, I have depended on Jim Falk for stimulating discussion and unconditional support. Anna and Michael Falk have enriched my life in immeasurable ways and, in good humour, accommodated their lives to those of academic parents. It is my hope that this book goes some way towards meeting a pressing need, namely the development of a body of contemporary theory for the textile art movement around the world. As students, lecturers, artists, curators, writers, critics and publishers, we all have a role to play in creating greater understanding of the medium.

The publisher wishes to acknowledge the support of Southern Arts, in association with Hampshire County Council, and in particular Paul Clough, David Kay, Keiren Phelan. Many thanks also to Diana Drummond, Susan Lordi Marker and Dennis Marker, Professor Anne Morrell, Paul Richardson at Oxford Brookes University, and Katharina Riegler.

CONTRIBUTORS

Dr Sue Rowley is Pro-Vice Chancellor (Research) at the University of Technology, Sydney, Australia, and formerly Professor and Head of the School of Art History and Theory in the University of New South Wales College of Fine Arts. Her interdisciplinary interests are indicated by her undergraduate majors in Sociology, Politics, Textiles and Art Theory, complemented by a PhD in cultural, visual and literary history. She writes and publishes widely on contemporary visual art and craft, and has curated international exhibitions of textiles and contemporary craft. She is President of Object-Centre for Contemporary Craft and is Editor of *Craft and Contemporary Theory*, published by Allen & Unwin.

Dr Hazel Clark is an Associate Professor in the School of Design, Hong Kong Polytechnic University. Her teaching and writing focuses on design theory with a special interest in textiles and dress, consumption and cultural identity. She is currently working on a book on the *cheung sam* (the female dress particularly associated with Hong Kong).

Wlodzimierz Cygan is one of Poland's most distinguished textile artists. A prize winner at the 2nd International Textile Competition, Kyoto, as well as at the 8th Weaving Triennial, Lodz, he is Editor of the magazine *Text and Textile: Fibre Art* (*Text i textil – sztuka wlokna*) and of the journal Fibers and Textiles in Eastern Europe. He runs a weaving studio at the Academy of Fine Arts, Gdansk and is Senior Lecturer in the Department of Constructed Textiles, Technical University of Lodz.

Jasleen Dhamija was invited by the Indian government to spearhead an initiative to revive traditional textiles and handicrafts in India. The success of this scheme has led to her being invited as consultant to a number of other international craft organisations, travelling extensively in the Middle East, Africa and South East Asia.

Janis Jefferies is Reader and Head of Textiles in the Department of Visual Arts, Goldsmiths College, University of London, UK. She studied Fine Art (England) and woven construction at the Academy of Fine Arts, Poland, under Magdalena Abakanowicz in the 1970s. She has exhibited internationally, curated exhibitions and written for many magazines worldwide. Her critical writing and studio work focuses on the relationship between text and textiles, gender and subjectivity, and photography and the real.

Doreen Mellor is an Indigenous Australian, her cultural origins being in the rainforest country of the Atherton Tableland in North Queensland. Immediate past Director of Flinders University Art Museum in Adelaide, she now works independently as a curator and arts manager in Canberra. For a period of four years, she was Visual Arts Manager and Curator at Tandanya National Aboriginal Cultural Institute, and has prepared major reports on Indigenous arts issues at national, state and community levels.

Margo Mensing is an artist and writer who lectures at Skidmore College, Saratoga Springs, NY, USA. One of America's foremost writers on textiles, she contributes to *Surface Design Journal, Fiber Arts* and other specialist publications.

Nima Poovaya-Smith was formerly Senior Keeper, International Arts, Bradford Art Galleries and Museums. She is currently Director of Arts, Yorkshire Arts.

Julián Ruesga Bono is an artist, working with textiles and digitalized images. His work is centred on the semanticity and social use of textiles and cultural intertextuality, and is exhibited in Europe and America. He is Director and Editor of *Arte/Facto*, and his writing is published regularly in exhibition catalogues and specialist magazines in Spain, Germany, United States, Australia and Argentina. He has been consultant and curator for various international exhibitions and has given courses, workshops and seminars on textiles and art in various centres and universities in Spain, Europe and Latin America.

Dr Diana Wood Conroy has a Bachelor of Arts (Honours) in Archaeology from the University of Sydney and a Doctor of Creative Arts from the University of Wollongong where she is Lecturer in Visual Arts. Her exhibition *Archaeologies: Structures of Time* with Sharon Marcus was shown in Portland USA, Sydney and Wollongong. She was curatorial adviser to Taipei Fine Arts Museum, Taiwan for the exhibition *Identities: Art from Australia*. She has been team manager and artist-in-residence to the Paphos Theatre excavation in Cyprus (with the University of Sydney) from 1996.

CONTENTS

LIST OF ILLUSTRATIONS

Colour Plates

CRAFT, CREATIVITY AND CRITICAL PRACTICE

Sue Rowley

Modernism: Creativity and the Conservatism of Craft

In recent years, a number of writers have pointed out that modernist thought and art positioned craft as the 'other' of art.[1] From the early twentieth century, craft was assumed to be dependent on tradition, and modern art was deeply concerned to break away from the shackles of tradition. Artists of the *avant-garde* movements fervently sought to 'make-it-new'. Craft represented the past. Hand production was understood not only to have been left behind – or rather, swept aside – by industrialisation, but skilled craft makers were seen as resistant to change, and this resistance was seen to underscore an essential conservatism in craft culture.

Particularly in the first half of the twentieth century, as both Andreas Huyssen and Raymond Williams have argued, the *avant-garde* movements were fired by a utopian vision and a radical politics underpinned by a belief in progress and, to use Huyssen's phrase, a technological imagination. Artists believed that, through their work, they could transform everyday life.[2] In place of hand-production, artists associated with the Russian *avant-garde* and the Bauhaus inspired the emerging profession of design with utopian conviction.[3] For many artists, the imagination was fired by the culture of technology, which they found dynamic and compelling. Visual languages associated with modernism utilised fragmentation, assemblage, spontaneity, chance and gesture. There seemed to be no need for the staid materiality of objects that testified to laboriously acquired skill and the 'there-ness' of the past.

As Rosalind's Krauss influential essay convincingly argues, modern artists saw themselves as the point of origin of their work. Originality in art, in the sense of being 'without antecedents', was inextricably tied to the notion of authorship.[4] As Krauss notes, this concept of originality is set up precisely in relation to tradition:

> The self as origin is safe from contamination by tradition because it possesses a kind of imaginary naiveté...The self as origin is the way an absolute distinction can be made between a present experienced *de novo* and a tradition-laden past.[5]

By contrast, craft practices seem too indebted to the past, and too lacking in spontaneity to produce 'original' objects.

Gloria Tamerre Petyarre (1997)
(Utopia Awely Batik Aboriginal Corporation)
azoic batik on silk
500 x 120cm

The originality of art was signified by the signature of the artist. The assumed and ascribed anonymity of artisans and craft practitioners appears to be derived from their lack of originality. Establishing name and signature of the artist has become a major strategy for gaining artworld acceptance for craft objects. In Australia, for example, Aboriginal artists who made batiks in the Utopia community and pots at Hermannsburg were known by collective and community-based labels, such as 'Utopian batiks' or 'Hermannsburg potters'. Over the last few years, however, the names of individual artists have been used and this coincides with the greater acceptance of their work into art collections and exhibitions.[6] In introducing the work of five contemporary folk and tribal artists of India, Jyotindra Jain distinguishes between the individuality of artists and the appearance of their signature on the artwork. 'If the artist's name was not inscribed on a work of art, it was not because his individuality as an artist was required to be eclipsed,' he writes.[7]

As the utopian vision of art as a transformative practice faded after the Second World War, the autonomy of the artwork and its separation from everyday life were emphasised.[8] The disinterestedness of the artist was mirrored by the detachment of the art object from the business of living. Apprehending the significance of the art object was understood to be an intellectual-aesthetic act, typically a contemplation of the object in an architectural context which 'whites-out' the noise of the world. Increasingly, the 'embeddedness' of craft objects in everyday life, as useful things, gifts, memoirs, came to connote a lack of detachment. Useful things, it seemed, could not communicate important insights into the human condition. The busy craft object, passing from hand to hand, acquired a patination of use rather than a provenance of value.

This view of craft has been tenacious. In his 1988 essay, 'The ideal world of Vermeer's little lacemaker', Peter Dormer argued that craft-makers are too absorbed in their work: craft practice 'banished' critical, speculative, interpretative or self-reflective thought.[9]

Whether we speak of the making, the makers or the objects, within modernist discourse the term 'craft' has carried connotations of conservatism and resistance to change. Held in the thrall of tradition, craft has appeared to be lacking in originality and impoverished as a signifying practice. In comparison with art, craft appears not only conservative, but craft practice seems to lack creativity. The twin values of originality and critical insight which underpinned modernist notions of creative artistic practice are not recognised in 'tradition-bound' craft practice.

The idea of creativity has had a rather chequered career. 'Imagination' would be a good alternative for the purposes of this discussion but, in the visual arts, 'imagination' has become too closely aligned with 'image'. This account is, nevertheless, indebted to Richard Kearney's excellent history of theories of imagination in *The Wake of Imagination: Ideas of Creativity in Western Culture*.[10]

Postmodernism: Critical Practice

Compared to modernist thought and art, postmodernism is predicated on weaker notions of creativity. The heroic aspirations of the modern world – authors, originality, progress – are greatly diminished. There are no originals in postmodernism: images are re-cycled and re-presented; repetition, copying and appropriation become hallmarks of postmodern practice. Richard Kearney writes:

> Right across the spectrum of structuralist, poststructuralist and de-constructionist thinking, one notes a common concern to dismantle the very notion of imagination. Where it is spoken of at all, it is subjected to suspicion or denigrated as an outdated humanist illusion.[11]

'The philosophical category of imagination,' Kearney notes, 'appears to be dissolving into an anonymous play of language'. Even so, postmodernism has its own language of creativity, evident in such phrases as 'experimental art', or 'the cutting edge' of contemporary practice. Kearney himself proposes a theoretical re-inscription of a postmodern ethical, critical, poetic imagination.[12]

In principal, postmodernism nurtures more positive attitudes than those of modernism towards craft. This, I would argue, is borne out also in more diverse and integrated art-world opportunities for contemporary craft practice. However, to the extent that postmodern notions of creativity emphasise representation over object, and bricolage over skill, these notions do not recuperate craft practice. Breaking down the opposition of high art and popular culture similarly opens up space for craft but, in fact, it is the culture of mass media, mass production and mass consumption that is the focus here. Artisan traditions and hand-technologies remain peripheral to the focal concerns of postmodern theory and practice.

Significantly, the legacy of modernism's radical utopianism is evident in the contemporary idea of art as critical practice. No longer confident in the capacity of art to transform life, many artists and critics retain a deep commitment to politically-engaged practice. Contemporary art is intended to offer interpretative and revelatory comment on social life. The current usage of terms like 'neo-avant-garde' and 'critical practice' suggests that the transformative project of historical *avant-garde* has not been abandoned. Emphasising the notion of a modernist tradition, Charles Harrison argues that 'modernism' does not refer solely to art practice but also to labelling a specific tradition and tendency in criticism.[13]

We should not underestimate the vitality of this critical and artistic tradition of modernism in shaping contemporary art's institutionalised practices. In some ways, the critical tradition has become uncoupled from the artistic tradition. Modern art seems 'historical' (pertaining to the past) in a way that is not the case with the critical practices of modernism, specifically those that define what objects and practices, and which artists, fall within its domain. In this sense, the on-going and unresolvable debate about the relationship between modernism and postmodernism ironically reinforces the idea of the modernist tradition, which, for earlier generations, would have seemed to be an oxymoron.

It has been difficult to write craft into the domain of critical practice and to gain acceptance for craft in the contemporary art milieu. This is precisely because there is a sense of lineage traced back from contemporary art through the radical *avant-garde* movements of the twentieth century to the moral-political world views of nineteenth-century art and so on. The ascribed conservatism of craft is pivotal to maintaining the radical traditions of art. Insufficient attention has been paid to this ascription. This may be because craft practitioners, writers, curators and theorists have been relatively comfortable with the assumption that craft practice is conservative, or because the significance of the assumption in the discursive formation of 'art' and 'craft' has not been recognised.

Poststructuralist theories have opened up a critical space for craft practice. The critique of authorship – the rejection of the authority of the artist – has thrown the emphasis on the negotiation that invests texts, artworks and objects with meaning. The autonomy of the artwork is undermined and the object is recognised as being embedded in cultural practices and contexts. The meaning and value of art is constituted through negotiation, not inherent in the artwork or the artist. Within poststructuralism, critical practice refers as much to the act of constituting meaning through 'reading texts' as to making meaningful objects.

Interesting, deconstructive poststructuralism goes some way to redress the malaise of creativity. Avoiding the heroic aspirations of modernism, poststructuralism nevertheless places great emphasis on chains of invention. Precisely, the absence of a definitive original makes room for intervention, innovation, re-invention, terms which imply a stronger concept of agency and creativity than postmodernism's other trademarks of representation and appropriation. In short, there are no originals, but we can conceive of forms of creative, inventive, imaginative practice without requiring origins or originals. A theoretical tool-kit is being assembled to re- conceptualise craft in relation to modernism's negative characterisation of crafts as conservative, lacking originality, and incapable of acting as a signifying practice.

Difference: Postcolonial Creativity and Craft

The notion of difference, derived from the work of Jacques Derrida, refuses to conceive of the world as coherent and singular, insisting instead on multiplicity and irreconcilable, irreducible differences in human experience and culture. It is this concept that has given much of the bite to postcolonialism. 'Difference' underscores the belated recognition that Euro-American modernity has not laid down the template for the experience of modernity by other peoples and in other lands. All modernisms are not essentially derivative of Euro-American modernism which, by the same token, can no longer be seen as a coherent, historically unilinear 'trajectory'. The multiplicities of differentiated historical experience and agency become important in the context of a heightened awareness of the current global re-configuration. In principal, the experiences of postcolonial modernities have become as significant as those of Euro-American imperial modernities in understanding the contemporary world.'[14]

At the same time, the ways in which these histories are recounted is subject of debate, contestation and innovation. The authority of history challenged, histories are understood now to be partial, constructed narratives which cannot substantiate a claim to be disinterested, unified or conclusive. Other, competing modes of narrating the past are explored, as Huyssen argues in his discussion of the current obsession with 'memory'. In this 'memory project', objects and belongings have acquired a complex and tangible presence as vehicles of memory and the means by which past experience is conveyed and mediated in the present.

Postcolonialism is built on a much more robust conceptualisation of creative practice. Its roots in literary practice and theory should not be overlooked. Postcolonialism is centred on the use of the language of colonial powers by colonised people to express their own local and specific experience. Language itself is transformed in the articulation of 'foreign' experiences and reflections. The notion of difference becomes a key, but this time authorship is strengthened: writers and artists can be understood as making meaningful objects, not simply objects from which meaning may be inferred by insightful readers and critics.[15]

In its attention to local histories and cultures, postcolonial practice frequently invokes traditions, especially those related to creative and symbolic practices such as storytelling, popular culture and craft. In spite of, or perhaps because of the centrality of language, resistance to the imposition of colonial culture and the re-forging of identity has emerged as a central theme of postcolonialism. So postcolonial artworks might invoke craft and might incorporate craft practices or objects as a means of delineating that which is indigenous, local and specific.

But, just as postcolonial writers take English (or Dutch or French) as their starting point, so many postcolonial artists take 'international' contemporary art as theirs. It is in this milieu that they seek to affirm the specificity of their historical and cultural experience. Clearly this has implications for craft practitioners and objects. Given the centrality of representation to both literature and visual art, postcolonial cultural production and studies tend to be under-pinned by theories of representation. For this reason, as Tim Barringer and Tom Flynn comment, debates about colonialism have paid scant attention to functional and non-functional three-dimensional objects. They note that there is 'a certain irony in this since the circulation of goods and the increase of trade was a primary underlying motivation for imperial expansion'.

It is one thing to invoke the craft and artisan cultural practices and traditions; it is quite another to over-write Euro-American traditions of delineating craft as 'not-art'. Craft can be used to signify non-Western and resistant modes of creative practice without actually being recognised as contemporary art, or as critical practice, on its own terms. Indeed, critically engaged, signifying practices within contemporary craft are, in a sense, both superfluous to the requirements of contemporary art, and redundant because the trajectory of traditional modernist art practices leaves no space for their inclusion.

The important thing to note here is that difference is never simply a priori, a pre-existing given which is re-presented in art and language. Rather, difference is produced. As Gerald Sider and Gavin Smith argue,

> ...we are not so much dealing with any abstract, historically static quality – distance, otherness, 'alterity' – but rather with processes of differentiation.[17]

These processes of differentiation, they continue, 'turn out to be based as much or more on closeness and intimacy as on any imagined (or more, desired) difference'. Art is one of the sites for producing, maintaining and containing difference. The concept of difference problematises the relationship of art and craft practices and objects by neither obscuring nor reifying points of difference and sameness. It also draws attention to the role of the art institutions in managing the processes of differentiation in material and visual culture.

Undoubtedly, the notion of difference has acted as a fulcrum in postcolonial critical cultural practice. But in the context of a globalising political economy, difference is not secured for critique. This point is made forcefully in a recent essay by Lawrence Grossberg. In the past, capitalism refused differences which restricted productivity; today it works by the production of difference itself.[18] But it is the form, not the content, of this ubiquitous difference that is produced: 'difference has been commodified'. Noting that capitalism produces difference 'at the level of expression', Grossberg comments that this 'obviously makes the current faith in difference as the site of agency and resistance problematic'. In recognising that difference is produced – and indeed, is produced within the institutions and conventions of international art – we acknowledge that this may signify both a creative activity and a curtailing of creativity.

Notwithstanding the ambivalence of the concept, difference lies at the heart of notions of creativity, imagination and innovation as they emerge in writing on cultural displacement and cultural contact. Much of the recent writing on diaspora, exile and travel, on cross-cultural contact, colonisation and exchange, and on translation and misreading, is suggestive of a renewed confidence in a human capacity for creative as well as critical agency. Take, for example, James Clifford's observation that 'cultural action, the making and remaking of identities, takes place in the contact zones, along the policed and transgressive intercultural frontiers of nations, peoples, locales'.[19]

Significantly, the subject of this new writing is still modernity, even though the focus has broadened from the imperial centres of Europe and America to encompass the rest of the world. 'What are the conditions for serious translation between different routes in an interconnected but not homogeneous modernity?', Clifford asks.[20] The leitmotifs of modernity – dynamism, accelerating pace of change, breakdown of traditions, severed connections, discovery of new worlds, inventions of new technologies – reinforce the perception that modernity is the impetus for creativity. And so it is. Nevertheless, the experience of modernity does not account for creativity per se. Jyotindra Jain makes this qualification:

> The notion of change in the artistic ethos...cannot always be comprehended by such broad and charged terms as 'modernisation',

'urbanisation' and 'commercialisation'. Some or all of them may be operative in given situations, in varying degrees and combinations, and still there may be a local interactive pattern of individual or collective cultural factors at work which may provide a resource to the artist.[21]

A similar reservation about the singularity of modernity in generating the conditions for change and creativity is expressed by Edward M. Bruner. He comments that societies have had to contend with situations of interaction between two or more cultures 'as part of the very conditions of human existence'.[22] Nicholas Thomas turns the modernity/innovation dialectic around to argue that 'Indigenous cultures have not necessarily been profoundly influenced by colonial culture'; that they are not necessarily radically transformed by, or resistant to modernisation; and that interacting cultures do not necessarily proceed along a path towards deeper mutual engagement, towards some kind of hybridity.[23]

Tradition

If creativity is implicitly theorised in terms of the dynamism of modernity or the frisson of difference, how is creativity in traditional cultures to be understood? In their influential essay on the 'invention of tradition', Eric Hobsbawm and Terence Ranger posit 'invariance' as the defining characteristic of tradition.[24] They contrast tradition with custom which, they say, 'does not preclude innovation and chance up to a point, though the requirement that it must appear compatible or even identical with precedent imposes substantial limitations on it'. Though custom gives any desired change (or resistance to innovation) the sanction of precedent, social continuity and natural law as expressed in history, it 'cannot afford to be invariant because even in "traditional" society, life is not so'.

In *The Invention of Tradition* Hobsbawm and Ranger present a series of case studies of 'invented traditions' of nineteenth and twentieth-century Britain. They define invented traditions as including those which are actually invented, constructed and formally instituted and 'those emerging in a less easily traceable manner within a brief and dateable period and establishing themselves with great rapidity'. These invented traditions attempt to structure social life as unchanging and invariant by establishing apparent continuity with a suitable past, frequently by the use of repetition. The context of these studies is modernity: invented traditions arise because 'new or dramatically transformed social groups, environments and social contexts called for new devices to ensure or express social cohesion and identity and to structure social relations' or because traditional forms of ruling 'grew more difficult or impracticable, requiring new methods of ruling or establishing bonds of loyalty'.

But is 'invariance' the defining characteristic of tradition? In fact, Hobsbawm and Ranger are inconsistent on this. Their use of the term implies a useful anthropological definition of tradition as 'a set of practices, normally governed by overtly or tacitly accepted rules and of a ritual or symbolic nature, which symbolise social cohesion, legitimate social institutions and inculcate certain values and norms of behaviour through reference to the authority of the past'. They acknowledge that 'even traditional *topoi* of genuine antiquity may have breaks in continuity' and that 'the strength and adaptability of genuine traditions is not to be confused with the invention of traditions. Where old ways are alive, traditions need neither to be revived nor invented'. The distinction between tradition and custom, then, seems not so clear-cut. As with custom, we could conclude that tradition is not invariant because life is not so.

If traditions are recognised as embedded in history, then the apparent differences between adaptation, revival and invention are undermined. Michael Taylor asks:

> Are the despoiling effects of recent changes fundamentally different from changes in past centuries? Are they the same kind of changes that have taken place elsewhere but are now occurring in more remote areas as those areas are 'discovered', allowing today's observers to record the changes first hand? Or have changes steadily been taking place everywhere with such force that we waste our grief in mourning the loss of remote and untouched traditions – since there are none.[25]

'How much change,' he asks, 'constitutes the loss of tradition versus the creative adaptation of a traditional form?'

Peter Osborne in *The Politics of Time: Modernity and Avant-Garde* describes as 'a form of temporalisation...distinguished by its apparent priorization of the past over both present and future'.[26] Consequently, 'the present presents itself as the site for the transmission of the past into the future' and 'the future is envisaged in the image of the past'. Osborne writes of tradition as a 'quasi-natural form' which is dependent on the physical proximity of the members of a community, and kinship as a model of social power:

Tradition shadows the biological continuity of generations at the level of social form. Anchoring ethics and politics to nature, it connects the idea of history to the life of the species.

For this reason, he concludes the primary medium of tradition is not self-consciousness, but 'the pregiven, unreflected and binding existence of social forms'. Thus, the idea of tradition, as a self-recognising practice, does not arise within those 'original' communities in which its presence is deeply naturalised. Rather, tradition, as an idea, is produced within modernity, and as its inescapable dialectical other:

> ...as a periodising concept, modernity marks out the time of the dialectics of modernity and tradition as competing, yet intertwined forms of historical consciousness, rather than that of a single temporal form, however abstract.

What is perceived as 'tradition' from the vantage of point of modernity is experienced as part of the natural order in those original communities which are positioned implicitly as 'outside history'.

In contrast to the argument for invariance advanced by Hobsbawm and Ranger, Osborne sees the possibility of change as structured into tradition through the necessity of repetition and its inherent insecurity. The necessity of repetition in order to secure continuity, he proposes, introduces the possibility of failure in transmission:

> ...the continuity of tradition requires a constant exercise of authority to combat the threat of betrayal inherent in its temporal structure.

Osborne adopts the language of failure and betrayal (even noting that the root of the term tradition – *tradere* – has other meanings related to betrayal and surrender). But possibility of 'failure' can also be seen as a site of resistance and creativity. This possibility, which is inherent in the temporal structure of tradition, does not rest solely on the cataclysmic upheavals of modernity, which nevertheless do exacerbate the 'threat of betrayal'.

Anthropologists Smadar Lavie, Kirin Narayan and Renato Rosaldo incorporate invention into the transmission of tradition, arguing that the 'healthy perpetuation of cultural traditions requires invention as well as rote repetition'. Far from representing this as a betrayal, they argue that creativity is 'always emergent' for two reasons: firstly, because younger generations always select from, elaborate upon, and transform the traditions they inherit; and secondly, because decisions to alter nothing received from the past will usually be thwarted because changing circumstances transform the meaning and consequences of dutifully repeated traditional actions.[27] Thus, creativity 'often dissolves, or perhaps more precisely redraws the boundaries of social institutions and cultural patterns'.

Taken together, then, creativity and critique may operate within tradition. In theorising innovation and tradition, temporality emerges as a central issue.

Temporalities

A further complication here is that there is no singular structure of temporality. We are accustomed to thinking of postmodernity (and now 'globalisation') in terms of multiple structures of temporality. Contemporary global experience is characterised by disjunctures in the structures and organisation of time. The Euro-American perception of historical time as unilinear and progressive is an artefact of Western modernity, and the apparent universality of this temporality has been challenged by the critique of progress, by global interpenetration of diverse cultural constructs of time, and by the impact of new technologies of communication and information cyberspace. As Andreas Huyssen comments in *Twilight Memories*:

> ...we have accumulated so many non-synchronicities in our present that a very hybrid structure of temporality seems to be emerging, one that has clearly moved beyond the parameters of two and more centuries of European-American modernity.[28]

Even so, multiplicities of temporal structures are not the sole province of modernity or postmodernity. As David William Cohen observes,

> There are, within the production of history, complexities of time and temporalities, in which the very harmonic of historical practice – a common sense of time – may cover or efface powerful and competing senses of time, temporality, and temporicity, between and within cultures, among social groupings, classes, and households, and within the experience of the individual.[29]

Within these temporal multiplicities, space is opened up for creative practice. Homi Bhabha and Andreas Huyssen have both drawn attention to this dynamic. For Huyssen, it is in the representational act that re-constitutes the remembered past in the present that is the basis of creativity. 'The fissure that opens up between experiencing an event and remembering it,' he writes, 'is a powerful stimulant for cultural and artistic creativity'.

Homi Bhabha's essay 'How newness enters the world' explores directly the questions of creativity and tradition.[30] His ideas on the 'in-between' spaces have acquired a currency in contemporary writing but the emphasis he places on creativity is worth reiterating here. Bhabha writes of the impetus for creativity that is formed in 'a new international space of discontinuous historical realities' and 'the interstitial passages and processes of cultural difference'. For Bhabha, cultural difference is the prime mover in the production of creativity, but difference is theorised in relation to temporal orders. His theorisation of difference invokes the notion of tradition. Tradition, consigned to the past within modern thought, is retrieved for the present: the past is 'restaged', and 'incommensurable cultural temporalities [are introduced] into the invention of tradition'. Thus, he writes that the 'borderline engagements of cultural difference...may confound our definitions of tradition and modernity':

> The borderline work of culture demands an encounter with 'newness' that is not part of the continuum of past and present. It creates a sense of the new as an insurgent act of cultural translation. Such an art...renews the past, refiguring it as a contingent 'in-between' space, that innovates and interrupts the performance of the present. The 'past-present' becomes part of the necessity, not the nostalgia, of living.[31]

Thus the apparent dichotomy of tradition and innovation, so significant in defining modernity, but of little use in defining tradition, is undermined.

Craft Temporalities and Mortal Lives

It is useful to think of craft in terms of multiple temporalities. This idea informs the theoretical discussion of the relationship between craft practice and 'living' tradition, on the one hand, and between the making of objects and their subsequent careers as objects of symbolic and practical use, on the other. Craft's temporalities are the time-spans involved in making and using objects embedded in ceremonial, symbolic and everyday practices. Thinking about craft in terms of temporality enables certain suggestive, recurring threads to be drawn between the objects and human (which is to say, mortal and social) lives.

Let us begin with Norman Bryson's observation that the forms of the ta-
bleware figured in still-life painting belong to a long cultural span that goes
back to pre-antiquity: 'The bowls, jugs, pitchers and vases with which the
modern viewer is familiar are all direct lineal descendants of series which
were already old in Pompeii'.[32] By contrast, Bryson writes, the culture of the
table 'displays a rapid, volatile receptivity to its surrounding culture in the
mode of inflecting its fundamental forms'. Thus, Bryson distinguishes two
rates of change:

> rapid – there is constant inflection of the objects under the influences
> of the fast-moving changes that occur in the spheres of ideology,
> economics, and technology; and slow – there is little actual innova-
> tion as a result of this influence.[33]

Bryson conceives of the culture of the table as 'an authentically self-deter-
mining level of material life', arguing that this 'slowest, most entropic level
of material existence' is inescapable because it is formed by 'the conditions
of creaturality'. In relation to textiles, a similar argument might be made for
clothing and 'coverings' (rugs, wall hangings, curtains, bedding, etc.). For
Bryson, human creaturality necessitates eating and drinking, and the objects
used for these inescapable activities are shaped around needs, functions and
capabilities of the human body. From shards of objects whose forms are
familiar and accessible, archaeologists infer cultures and histories of past
worlds.

Like enduring forms of vessels and clothing shaped to the human body,
the acquisition of skill takes time.[34] It was precisely this investment of time
in acquiring skill – and the economic power that skilled workers could exercise by virtue of that investment – that the nineteenth and twentieth-century
industrialists sought to undercut through re-organisation of production and
the use of technologies. The long duration associated with acquiring craft
skills could not easily be assimilated into the rhetoric of modern art, with its
insistence on newness, spontaneity and ever-faster turn-around of ideas and
their visual articulation. Unlike eating and drinking, the acquisition of skills
is not an 'inescapable condition of creaturality': humans have a capacity for
skill which may never be realised. And increasingly, it appears that skills in
making things take too much time to acquire through practice.

There are other durations and rhythms associated with the making and
the using of objects. These, too, are evocative of human activities and bodies,
sociability, and ultimately, mortality. The rhythms of making, which Walter
Benjamin sees the formative context for story-telling, are the heart-beats of

human sociability. Is it romantic to suggest that the temporalities of craft are somehow bound up with those of the human body and social life? Possibly. But the suggestion itself quietly, insistently intrudes itself into shared perceptions of craft through literature, and theoretical and speculative writing. 'Craftsmanship is a sign that expresses society...as shared physical life,'writes Octavio Paz; 'it transforms a utensil into a sign of participation'.[35]

Paz compares the duration of the craft object to the 'air-conditioned eternity' of the art object and the 'trash-bin' transience of the industrial object. Whilst the artwork is not usually (literally) worn out by our observation of it, we invest meaning in everyday objects through the deepening familiarity of use: they wear out as we get to know them. In Biographical Objects, Janet Hoskins draws on a similar distinction made by Violette Morin between public commodities and 'biographical objects'. She comments that 'the biographical object grows old, and may become worn and tattered along with the life span of its owner, while the public commodity is eternally youthful and not used up but replaced':

> ...the biographical object limits the concrete space of its owner and sinks its roots deeply into the soil. It anchors the owner to a particular time and place...it 'imposes itself as the witness of the functional unity of its user, his or her everyday experience made into a thing'.[36]

As Paz observes, 'the work of craftsmanship is the pulse of human time':

> Craftwork teaches us to die, and by doing so teaches us to live.

From a very different starting point, Andreas Huyssen picks up a related theme to argue that we are living through a transformation of the structure of temporality in which the relationship of past, present and future is being transformed. Huyssen's argument in relation to the current obsession with memory could be extended to the conceptualisation of craft. He suggests that 'the memory boom' is:

> ...a reaction formation of mortal bodies that want to hold on to their temporality against a media world spinning a cocoon of timeless claustrophobia and nightmarish phantasms and simulations.[37]

If there is a thread connecting craft to human time-spans, rhythms and mortality, then the making and using of material objects is also an expression of 'the basic human need to live in extended structures of temporality, however they may be organised'. Further, the conceptualisation of craft in terms of temporalities has reinforced the social embeddedness of craft. The table for Bryson, the story-telling for Benjamin, the fiesta for Paz: not only are the objects and their making inherently social, but they appear to constitute the social world.

This is why the connection between craft and tradition has been so tenacious. Like tradition, craft is deeply naturalised as an articulation of human mortality and sociability. Osborne's comment that tradition 'connects the idea of history to the life of the species' could apply equally well to the concept of craft.

And this is why craft was such an anathema to modernism. A different, incompatible concept of nature underpins modernist art, as evidenced by its intense interest in the unconscious and insanity, and in its conceptualisation of the primitive, the child and Woman. Stripped of the coercive bindings of civilisations, modernist thought conceived of human-in-nature as 'outside society' as well as 'outside history'. The alienation that Marx saw as resulting precisely from modernity is mirrored and displaced. While the spontaneity and un-self-consciousness of 'outsider art' could be celebrated for its freedom from rationality, its incorporation as art was effected by the self-reflective, critical practices of modernism. Within modern aesthetic-critical thought, human nature was conceived of as being in opposition to human sociability. Craft and tradition, by contrast, represented a competing conceptualisation of 'the human condition'. Equivalent in their lack of self-awareness and critical distance, outsider art was the expression of an unshackled mentality, whereas craft was represented as bound by unreflecting, invariant habit.

Creating Meaning

Many artists, including installation artists and textile artists, invoke craft precisely to reflect critically on the questions of social formation and temporal experience in the emerging context of a global political economy formed in conjunction with the new information technologies. Craft is employed as a sign of alternative possibilities for social identity and community, usually grounded in a sense of historical depth, but without acceding to the authority of history to shape the present. In this sense, craft functions as a sign of an alternative, community-based creativity, resistant to the modernist notion of the heroic genius.

In her anthropological study of 'biographical objects', Janet Hoskins suggests that possessions to which value and significance are attached can act as 'surrogate selves', endowed with the personal characteristics of their owners and used to 'reify characteristics of personhood that must then be narratively organised into an identity'. Thus, an object can become 'a way of knowing oneself through things'.

> The imagination works on objects to turn commodities, gifts, or ordinary utilitarian tools into sometimes very significant possessions, which draw their power from biographical experiences and the stories told about these.[38]

Hoskins summarises differences between Kodi exchange objects and modern consumer objects in terms of their investment in form and in work, value placed on age rather than novelty and their exchange histories. She notes, too, that in modern industrial societies, objects imbued with particular personal significance tend to be more directly representational. The way in which Hoskins handles the relationship between self and object resonates strongly with the perception of many craft-makers that objects may validly act as vehicles by which identity and memory may be organised and expressed. From this perspective, objects are imbued with meaning through use and, in turn, they enable personal and cultural experiences to be constituted as meaningful. This does suggest a conceptualisation of creativity different from that of the critical tradition of art, with its strong emphasis on representation and reflection. Through objects, identities are forged. As jeweller Susan Cohn has argued, this insight into the symbolic function of objects is invested in their craft manufacture.

The relationship between craft and creativity is re-conceptualised, beyond simply acknowledging that critical representational practices which fulfil a symbolising function do not exclude craft practices. More inclusively, Lavie, Narayan and Rosaldo define creativity as 'human activities that transform existing cultural practices in a manner that a community or certain of its members find of value'. Thus, 'activities that induce creativity at times are... set apart in special spheres', but they are also at times 'integrated into the mun-dane arenas of everyday life'. Significantly they see creativity as inherant in both individuals and social situations. Always emergent, erupting at unpredictable times and on unexpected occasions, this definition does not require that we dismantle the 'special sphere' – art – in order that other creativities, in other arenas of social life, might be conceivable. The contemporary conjunction of creativity and critical practice is retained while the possibility, and limitations of transformative practice, are asserted.

The Essays

Cross-cultural dialogue and critical creative practice are key themes in this book of essays which share a deep commitment to contemporary textile art. Writers from many countries and continents explore relationships between tradition and innovation in the art and craft of textile and fibre production. Many of the writers are themselves artists who work with textile and fibre media; others are curators, historians and writers. Most of the contributors work across these apparently discrete practices. Artists Wlodzimierz Cygan and Julián Ruesga Bono both edit journals, *Text i Textil* (Poland) and *Arte/facto* (Spain), respectively. Other artists – Diana Wood Conroy, Margo Mensing and Janis Jefferies, for example – are widely known also for their writing about textile and fibre art. And those who research and write also curate exhibitions: Nima Poovaya-Smith and Doreen Mellor. All of the contributors, in one way or another, are also teachers: some, like Hazel Clark, work within universities; others, like Jasleen Dhamija work independently of the formal institutional framework.

This shared commitment, these differences and similarities, and these multiple practices, then, lie at the heart of this collection of essays which re-thinks tradition and innovation, in relation to the past and the present, and in relation to modernity and the contemporary moment.

Notes

1. A good review of the negative impact of modernism on craft is given by Terry Smith, 'Craft, Modernity and Postmodernity', *Craft and Contemporary Theory* (ed. Sue Rowley), Allen and Unwin, Sydney, 1997, pp. 18–28; see also Paul Greenhalgh, 'The history of craft', The Culture of Craft (ed. Peter Dormer), Manchester University Press, Manchester and New York, 1997, pp. 20–52; Sue Rowley, 'Mind over matter? Reading the Art/Craft debate', *West* vol.1, no. 1,1989, pp. 3–7.

2. Huyssen, A., *After the Great Divide: Modernism, Mass Culture, Postmodernism*, Indiana University Press, Bloomington and Indianapolis,1986; Raymond Williams, *The Politics of Modernism: Against the New Conformists* (ed. Pinkney, T.), Verso, London and New York, 1989; see also, Edward Timms and Peter Collier, *Visions and Blueprints: Avant Garde Culture and Radical Politics in Early Twentieth-Century Europe*, Manchester University Press, Manchester, 1988.

3. For further discussion on design and radical culture, see Michael Collins, *Towards Postmodernism: Design Since 1851*, British Museum Publications, London, 1987; Adrian Forty, *Objects of Desire: Design and Society Since 1750*, Thames and Hudson, London,1995; Jonathan M. Woodham, *Twentieth Century Design*, Oxford University Press, Oxford, 1997; Isabelle Anscombe, *A Woman's Touch: Women in Design from 1860 to the Present Day*, Virago, London, 1984; Torsten Bröhan and Thomas Berg, *Avantgarde Design 1880–1930*, Taschen, Köln, 1995; Abbott Gleason, Peter Kenez and Richard Stites, *Bolshevik Culture: Experiment and Order in the Russian Revolution*, Indiana University Press, Bloomington and Indianapolis, 1985.

4. Rosalind E. Krauss, 'The Orginality of the Avant-Garde', *The Originality of the Avant-Garde*

and Other Modernist Myths, The MIT Press, Cambridge and London, 1987.

5. Ibid., p. 157.
6. Compare, for example, two early publications: Jenny Green, *Utopia: Women, Country and Batik*, Utopia Women's Batik Group, Alice Springs, 1981, and Peter Brockensha, *The Pitjantjatjara and their Crafts*, Aboriginal Arts Board, Australia Coujncil, Sydney, 1975, with recent publications on contemporary Abonginal art. (Also see Doreen Mellor's essay in this volume.)
7. Jyotindra Jain, 'Introduction', *Other Masters: Five Contemporary Folk and Tribal Artists of India* (ed. Jyotindra Jain), Crafts Museum and The Handicrafts and Handlooms Exports Corporation of India, New Delhi, 1998, p. 9.
8. See Andreas Huyssen, 'The Hidden Dialectic', *After the Great Divide*, pp. 3–15.
9. Peter Dormer, 'The ideal world of Vermeer's little lacemaker', *Design After Modernism: Beyond the Object* (ed. John Thackara), Thames and Hudson, London, 1988, p. 135.
10. Richard Kearney, *The Wake of Imagination: Ideas of Creativity in Western Culture*, Hutchinson, London, Melbourne, Auckland & Johannesburg, 1988.
11. Kearney, *The Wake of Imagination*, p. 251.
12. For useful discussions of postmodernism, in this context, see: Linda Hutcheon, *The Politics of Postmodernism*, Routledge, London and New York, 1989; Linda Hutcheon, *A Poetics of Postmodenism: History, Theory*, London and New York, 1988; Hans Bertens, *The Idea of the Postmodern: A History*, Routledge, London and New York, 1995.
13. Charles Harrison, *Modernism*, Tate Gallery Publishing, London, 1997, p. 21.
14. An exemplary study in non-Western modernism is John Clark, *Modern Asian Art*, Craftsman House, Sydney, 1998.
15. See, for example, Chris Tiffin and Alan Lawson, *Describing Empire: Post-colonialism and Textuality*, Routledge, London and New York, 1994; Iain Chambers and Lidia Curti (eds), *The Post-Colonial Reader: Common Skies, Divided Horizons*, Routledge, London, 1996.
16. Tim Barringer and Tom Flynn (eds), *Colonialism and the Object: Empire, Material Culture and the Museum*, Routledge, London and New York,1998, p. 3.
17. Gerald Sider and Gavin Smith (eds), *Between History and Histories: The Making of Silences and Commemorations*, University of Toronto Press, Toronto, Buffalo, London, 1997, p. 9.
18. Lawrence Grossberg, 'The space of culture, the power of space', Chambers and Curti, p. 184.
19. James Clifford, Routes: *Travel and Translation in the Late Twentieth Century*, Harvard University Press, Cambridge and London,1997, p. 7.
20. Clifford, *Routes*, p. 13.
21. Jain, *Other Masters*, p. 13.
22. Edward M. Bruner, 'Creative persona and the problem of authenticity', *Creativity/Anthropology* (eds. Smadar Lavie, Kirin Narayan and Renato Rosaldo), Cornell University Press, Ithaca and London, 1993, p. 323.
23. Nicholas Thomas, 'Introduction', Nicholas Thomas and Diane Losche (eds), Double Vision: Art Histories and Colonial Histories in the Pacific, Cambridge University Press, Cambridge, New York and Melbourne, 1999, p. 13.
24. Eric Hobsbawn and Terence Ranger (eds), 'Introduction', *The Invention of Tradition*, Cambridge University Press, Cambridge, New York and Melbourne, 1997 [1983], pp. 1–14.
25. Paul Michael Taylor (ed.), *Fragile Traditions: Indonesian Art in Jeopardy*, University of Hawaii Press, Honolulu, 1994, p. 6.
26. Peter Osborne, *The Politics of Time: Modernity and Avant-Garde*, Verso, London and New York,1995, p. 127.
27. Smadar Lavie, Kirin Narayan and Renato Rosaldo (eds), *Creativity/Anthropology*, Cornell University Press, Ithaca and London, 1993, p. 5.
28. Andreas Huyssen, *Twilight Memories: Marking Time in a Culture of Amnesia*, Routledge, New York and London, 1995, p. 8.

29. David William Cohen, 'Further thoughts on the production of history', Gerald Sider and Gavin Smith, p. 302.
30. Homi Bhabha, 'How newness enters the world: postmodern space, postcolonial times and the trials of cultural translation', *The Location of Culture, London and New York*, Routledge, 1994, pp. 171–197.
31. Bhabha, 'Introduction', *The Location of Culture*, p. 2.
32. Norman Bryson, *Looking at the Overlooked: Four Essays on Still Life Paintings*, Reaktion Books, London, 1990, p. 13.
33. Bryson, *Looking at the, Overlooked*, p. 13.
34. Jeff Taylor, *Tools of the Trade: The Art and Craft of Carpentry*, Chronicle Books, San Francisco, 1996; Malcolm McCullough, *Abstracting Craft: The Practised Digital Hand*, TheMIT Press, Cambridge and London, 1996.
35. Octavio Paz, 'Seeing and using: art and craftsmanship', *Convergences: Essays on Art and Literature* (transl. Lane, H.) Bloomsbury, London, 1990, p. 60.
36. Janet Hoskins, *Biographical Objects: How Things Tell the Stories of People's Lives*, Routledge, New York and London, 1998, p. 8.
37. Andreas Huyssen, *Twilight Memories*, p. 9
38. Janet Hoskins, *Biographical Objects*, p. 196.

AUSTRALIAN INDIGENOUS TEXTILES: FACILITATING RADICAL EXCHANGE

Doreen Mellor

I think of textiles as the ameliorating layer between us, as living human creatures, and that other living creature – the earth. We are wonderfully compatible and complementary, ourselves and the earth, even symbiotic on many levels, but the mitigating layers of fibre between varying surface textures and tensions have made the relationship more sympathetic. Textiles – fibre processed to suit human needs – have been a companionable part of life for so long in so many ways and in every cultural situation imaginable, that I sometimes contemplate and marvel at the number of times the earth could have been wrapped in them, Christo-like, since human beings began to work with them.

But textiles, perhaps belying their longstanding and collective mediating role, are often found in the most assertive and transformative of paradigms. In Australian Indigenous cultures, a number of textile initiatives have come to signify the insistence of these peoples on designing the interface with Australian settler cultures, on their own terms. This authoritative stance in no way diminishes the other aspect of textile production, in both the commercial and artistic spheres, as a means of facilitating enlightened dialogue between the two. In fact, the degrees of both assertiveness and conciliation embedded within modern Indigenous textile practice in Australia are – if not infinite – certainly difficult to measure.

One of the most dynamic textile statements to hit the interface between settler and indigenous cultures here, was the Aboriginal flag, designed some years ago by Aboriginal artist Harold Thomas, and taken up as a powerful symbol for Aboriginal people, of their human rights, and of the strong spirit which sustains the culture. So politically charged has the flag become, that when the young Cathy Freeman combined it with the Australian flag after winning an athletics gold medal at the 1994 Commonwealth Games in Vancouver, she was censured by Australian athletics officialdom. This reprimand ignored the other non-political role of the flag – the one which underpinned the action

– as a call to the spirit of Aboriginal people everywhere, for pride and joy in their achievements and in their culture. The incident, with its front page, full-colour news stories across the country, and passionate statements issued from Prime Minister to student representative, was a model for the diversity of attitudes to the cultural interface between settlers and Indigenes in Australia. Textiles, in the form of a cloth flag, played a key role in this issue. Despite a profile which is usually low key and inconspicuous, the presence of textiles is universal (perhaps mandatory!). What can happen without them?

Ada Bird Petyarre
Utopia Awely Batik Aboriginal Corporation (Australia)
batik demonstration
Parc de la Villette, Paris, 1998

The long history of Australia's Indigenous peoples includes as intimate a relationship with fibre and textile as any other culture. Although differing from Western cultures in the approach to apparel, Aboriginal and Torres Strait Islander people were nevertheless delighted with and wholly engaged with fibre as both shelter, clothing and codified artefact. Before and since European settlement, most Aboriginal cultures manufactured fibre objects for uses as ceremonially significant as Christian cultures might regard Papal garb at Easter. Indeed, many fibre objects are not only used symbolically in ceremony, but continue to be regarded as Ancestor Beings, endowed with living spirit.

In Arnhem Land, around Australia's northern shores and hinterland, major creator figures are closely associated with fibre container forms. Ancestral Beings carried sacred objects, including conical mats and dilly bags, which were intimately connected with the birth of their children, as they travelled across the land. Their actions changed the landscape, producing sacred sites and significant landmarks which continue to be known to contemporary Indigenous people of these areas.[1] The present-day models of these ancestral containers, twined, looped and coil bundled, are at once important ceremonial objects, useful items and a way to engage with market forces.

Two modalities have traditionally characterised the fibre practice of Australian Indigenous people: the use of form and its intrinsic rhythms as a powerful and unaccompanied aesthetic element; and the use of colour or materials other than those provided by the base fibre itself, applied or attached to its surfaces as a way to enhance it and to embody layers of meaning.[2]

The fibre objects of Arnhem Land, for instance, have usually been enhanced by colour. Applied ochre colours, coloured feathers or other kinds of fibre twined into the objects are used for ceremonial purposes to express the excitement, shimmer and dazzle of specialness or 'occasion'.

In these northern cultures, both women and men work with fibre, making objects which range in size from monumental fish traps, woven from vine stems, to feathered and ochred arm bands (in the Burarra language – *nganybak*) Open-weave round mats such as the one made by Minnie Marabachiba and included in the exhibition *Maningrida: the Language of Weaving* are coloured with dye from the roots of native plants, or even the laundry 'blue bag' introduced by missionaries. Small twined carrying bags are made with dyed fibre, and ceremonial pieces are coloured in various other ways: ochre is painted onto the piece after it is made, or strips of coloured cloth and brilliantly coloured feathers are woven into the work. In the Burarra/Gunartpa language alone there are many names for these varieties of 'dilly' bag – *jerrk, galaburdok, bulupurr, mun-bolo* and many more – each describing a decorative feature, the material it is twined from, or an aspect of its use.

In other parts of Australia, it is the structure of the fibre object which makes the most emphatic statement: these forms include the traditional North Queensland bi-cornual basket, where the use of lawyer cane strips endows works with particular precision and clarity. The swishy, springy nature of lawyer cane led to its being part of the equipment in Queensland Education Department schools well into the 1960s. The baskets made with this cane were used by Aboriginal people also as a corrective device, but in a less menacing context than that of the corporal punishment meted out under the auspices of colonial rule in Queensland. Bi-cornual baskets, as well as being extraordinary in form, were also useful filters. Filled with toxic seeds and other plant material which could only be used as food after an extensive soaking and washing process, they were set in the fast-flowing streams which abounded in the tropical north, and left for an appropriate period of time. Their construction allowed the free flow of water through the cane strips, so that the material inside could undergo the required transformation.

There are also examples from Ngarrindjeri culture around the great Murray River in the south of the continent, where dense coil bundled objects make a statement about the challenges posed by this environment. Here, the cold wet winters have always demanded effective provisions for shelter. The abundance of plant material has ensured a rich array of fibre items, with extensive use of the water sedge *Cyperus gymnocaulos* which appears to have been an important material used by people from the Lower Murray, Lakes, Coorong area and the Murray River from Murray Bridge to the South Australian border, in both food retrieval and ceremonial contexts.[3] These objects all display a wonderful sculptural quality, only rarely enhanced by the use of other colourings or fibre in their construction. The decorative elements incorporated within woven objects of these areas mostly relate to the ways the coils are positioned. The hypnotic spiral form in some items will be repeatedly interrupted by looped openings, which eventually produce a stiff, lacy pattern.

The prevalence of one or the other of these two ways of working has usually had its origin in location and culture, rather than as a result of individual preference alone – the environment playing a major role in the development of characteristic ways of working. Nevertheless, within the self-imposed boundaries of cultural alliance, individual fibre practitioners exercised their options for creative self-expression and choice of approach and continue to do so today. Shaping fibre directly, working spatially, is a continuation of longstanding practices in Australian Indigenous cultural expression, engaging both men and women as part of a historical cultural openness to individual innovation and expression which provides the important foundation for the involvement of Indigenous artists in contemporary art practice.

Such fibre practice can be seen as a vehicle for active cultural exchange – in postcolonial times, a much more frequent event now than in the past, when the exchange was more often *de facto* than planned or even acknowledged. The use of various motifs from Indigenous culture – such as the ubiqitous boomerang form applied to everything from teatowels to doyleys – was widespread until recently. It is just a short time since the ownership of such symbols has been acknowledged and the dynamic of permission and reciprocity embedded in their use. In the same way, various Indigenous fibre practices filtered into the lexicon of non-Indigenous use, without the courtesy of identification. Conversely, a number of Western fibre and textile processing and making techniques were also imposed on Indigenous communities, usually in circumstances where local people were being encouraged or compelled to relinquish their own cultural activity, language and indigenous identity – so activities such basketmaking which adapted traditional forms to more acceptable Western usages, or rugmaking, with its overtones of a Western oriented domesticity, were encouraged. Such activity was not regarded as part of an exchange, but as a necessary educative process for people regarded as unenlightened, though exchange undoubtedly occurred. During Australia's precolonial history, there were various interchanges between Indigenous Australians and other cultures, especially those involving northern coastal areas proximal to the Indonesian islands. In Aboriginal paintings on bark and rock, there are many visual references to Macassan seafarers, and a number of cultural innovations can be traced to this contact with a nearby culture. In recent times, many Indigenous and non-Indigenous fibre practitioners have understood and enjoyed the reciprocity afforded by both spontaneous and planned trading of information.

Models for cultural dialogue and exchange, using work with fibre as a basis, are many and varied. Aboriginal fibre practitioners such as Ellen Trevorrow, as well as exhibiting widely both nationally and internationally, spend many hours teaching traditional techniques to interested beginners, both non-Indigenous and Indigenous. Artists and curators have entered into project situations where such exchange has been the focal energising force. Exhibitions have been arranged to highlight exchanges which have already taken place quietly, unacknowledged and sometimes without the full knowledge even of the participants. Such a situation was addressed by Aboriginal curator Kerry Giles in an exhibition titled *Two Countries, One Weave*, which explored the circumstances resulting from the intervention of Greta Matthews, the daughter of a missionary who worked at the turn of the century on a Murray River settlement. This young woman took a traditional coiling technique from the south to the north of the continent, where it has become part of the fibre practice of the host cultures in Arnhem Land. Coiled work in the north, however, has taken on an entirely different look, due to the brilliantly coloured plant dyes used to enhance the fibre forms – a reflection of the decorative application of ochre which preceded the use of dyes – and thought to be an outcome of the use of metal utensils brought by Westerners to the area.

The continuity of fibre traditions in Arnhem Land and other northern communities such as Peppimenarti and Wadeye allowed Indigenous people working with introduced techniques and technologies to confidently adapt, explore and change them over a long period of time, creating a range of basket structures which diverged from those traditionally created in these locations. Whilst the new forms and colours were being experimented with, traditional functions were still being fulfilled by the production of the classical fibre vessels and other objects relating to ceremony as well as daily activity.

A different story was to unfold in the south, where few cultural practices were able to be continued, and where many practices which depended on maintenance of language, ceremony and the cultural identity of communities dissolved. The creation of fibre objects as an integral and powerful part of the cultural life of peoples from the Coorong and Murray River systems gradually disappeared, until just a few women elders retained knowledge of the techniques used in those areas. This precious information was passed on to a small group of younger women, some of whom felt a strong custodianship responsibility towards the maintenance of fibre traditions. One artist in particular – Ellen Trevorrow – has developed her practice around the cherished familiarity of heritage items which survived colonial impact. Much knowledge has been added to the teaching given by Ngarrindjeri elders about fibre, by the resources made available from the archives and collection of the South Australian Museum. Remarkable footage is held on film of the collecting and processing of fibre, by Milerum (known also by his Western name, Clarence Long), an elder who worked closely with Norman Tindale at the South Australian Museum, in order to preserve at least some of the knowledge held by Ngarrindjeri people of his time.

Decoration and enhancement of processed textile surfaces has become widespread as a means of creative and cultural expression for Australian Indigenous people, and a number of centres have had a longstanding and formal involvement with introduced textile techniques. In the remote northern desert regions of South Australia, Ernabella Arts was established in 1948, and throughout the 1950s and 1960s women from the community of Ernabella engaged with various textile-based craft activities. Three women – all of whom later became well known as artists – travelled to Jogjakarta in 1975, to study at the Batik Research Centre, introducing this technique to their own community. Since then, walka – the designs of Ernabella based on traditional Pitjanjatjara women's practices of *milpatjunanyi* (story-telling accompanied by the drawing of designs in sand) and body painting for *inma* (ceremony) have been translated into batik images on silk. Spectacular pieces have been produced over the years, many of them being acquired by both public and private collections in Australia and overseas. In 1991, the Open Media Section of the national Aboriginal and Torres Strait Islander Art Awards in Darwin was won by Daisybell Kulyuru for her batik on silk. Batik and other dyeing techniques continue to form an important part of the fabric-designing activity of women artists at Ernabella, and a basis for diversification into other textile-based design activity.[4]

Another community well known for its dyed textiles is Utopia, north east of Alice Springs in the Northern Territory. During the late 1970s art programme were set in place, and batik dyeing techniques were used to articulate some of the designs based on *awelye*, or women's ceremonial knowledge, and the body designs associated with related ceremonial activity.[5] A small number of men also became involved in producing batik lengths, and to the present day continue to work with the medium. A number of Utopia women artists have become particularly well known as painters, having begun their artistic careers through batik workshops. Perhaps the most iconic of these is Emily Kngwarreye, whose work was honoured posthumously in a major retrospective exhibition presented by the Queensland Art Gallery, and toured to the major state and national galleries in eastern Australia.

In 1994 ten Utopia artists travelled to Jogjakarta, to engage in a workshop at Brahma Tirta Sari Batik Studio, which has pioneered the use of the hand-held copper stamp – *tjap* or *cap* – as a fine art medium. Work produced by the Utopia artists – two non-Indigenous Australian artists, and Indonesian-based artists Agus Ismoyo and Nia Filam – was incorporated in the exhibition *Hot Wax*, curated by Margie West for the Museum and Art Gallery of the Northern Territory.[6] In this group of works, the figurative imagery of the Utopia artists uses personal totemic images applied with brush and *tjanting*, alongside the *tjap* designs.

Another early textile printing venture – still a landmark operation in Aboriginal textile production – was Tiwi Designs, established after fabric printing workshops were held on Bathurst Island north of Darwin in 1969.[7] Tiwi Designs used designs which were created by men, for the most part, and it was men who worked the commercially sized screens. In more recent years Bima Wear, a women's cooperative, was also set up in the small community of Ngui. The distinctive and confident designs created by Tiwi people are applied to print making of all kinds, using motifs informed by traditional narratives. Printing on fabric has been particularly successful, with designs incorporating strong repeating motifs similar to those applied during ceremony on Pukamani poles and bodies.

The artists of Ernabella, Utopia and Bathurst Island have continued to develop their flourishing enterprises, and have been joined by many other diverse groups – sometimes in conjunction with remote art centres, and sometimes as dedicated textile design initiatives. A number of textile artists independently produce printed or dyed textiles for commercial or exhibiting purposes, and numerous education and training facilities engage with textile design and printing. These are most often Training and Further Education (TAFE) facilities, but there are also university faculties which have developed programmes specifically for Australian Indigenous students to explore various mediums, including textiles and fibre of different kinds. Some of the most well known of these include the programme at Cairns TAFE in North Queensland, the extensive art school programme at Griffith University in Brisbane, and the course offered by Taoundi, the Aboriginal College in Adelaide.

There are Australian Indigenous artists who have graduated from mainstream art schools, and whose textile work is held in national collections. Sydney artist Bronwyn Bancroft springs to mind, or north Queensland Thanaquith artist and educator Thancoupie, known more widely for her ceramic output. Bancroft underwent tertiary art training in the national capital, Canberra, and was instrumental in establishing Boomalli Aboriginal Artists Cooperative in Sydney, along with a number of other urban-based artists. Although her current output consists mainly of watercolour and acrylic paintings, her printed designs on fabric are held in high regard. Thancoupie's ceramic work is incised with motifs which embody cultural narrative. Sculptural form is enhanced by the coherence and tautness of these linear decorative elements, which translate in an eminently satisfying way, to repeated designs on fabric.

Textiles are used in diverse ways by artists working in studio environments. Judy Watson, an artist who has worked in a number of international situations, uses the canvas to which she applies paint and chalk, as textile. It is rolled and hung directly onto walls, rather than undergoing the stretching and framing process which would remove its portability and pliancy as a material. Watson works in an urban environment, but her work often refers to the north west Queensland country which holds the key to her cultural identity.

Fiona Foley is another artist whose working environment reflects her

Western-based art training. A member of the Badtjala language group from Thoorgine – Fraser Island – she lives nearby on the mainland, and constantly references the fragmented culture of the Badtjala people in her work. One of he installations, 'Ephemeral Spiral', was included in the exhibition *Ceremony, Identity and Community*, shown at the South African National Gallery in Cape Town in early 1999. This work comprises a group of blue cloth bags hung flat against the wall, each with a spiral form appliquéd to the side which faces outwards to the viewer. The spiral form is a reference to the large shells which were used in so many ways as part of the cultural activity of this coastal people, and mark her work as part of that cultural environment. Foley makes a personal statement here, which is both wistful and acerbic, about the absence of transmitted skills in making fibre objects such as dilly bags.

In addition to the initiatives of individual artists, there are one-off and *ad hoc* situations where project grants or special initiatives often result in the production of vibrant work. Some of these occur in remote communities, or in cities where remote artists visit to make use of facilities unavailable in the bush. However, textile printing also happens in unexpected places, where groups of Aboriginal or Torres Strait Island people – through unemployment programmes, or club activity – are presented with the opportunity to engage with the medium, and produce what can only be described as treasures. I remember in Sydney a few years ago, attending a Survival concert, the an-nual (alternative) Australia Day celebration organised by New South Wales communities, and being both taken aback and delighted to find amongst the many craft stalls a huge table full of printed textiles of every rich and varied hue and design possible. I was even more astonished to find that it wasn't the output of some highly organised commercial or artistic venture, but a group of women at Redfern, making excellent use of the facilities provided through a Community Development Employment Programme (CDEP).

Alongside – and in many cases connected with – the proliferation of art centres managed by Aboriginal people, these textile initiatives metaphori-cally fly the flag, asserting with their culturally based design elements an authoritative presence in contemporary Australian society.

Contemporary Australian Indigenous textile art uses a language which is at once aesthetic, functional, conceptual and explicitly cultural. It is because of this multiplicity of levels that it plays a role which has become increasingly important in the exchange between settler and Indigenous cultures in Australia, within the visual arts. This exchange is no longer a simple trade of inforrnation in order to enhance understanding, but has become a crucible where values from each culture are incorporated in the other. The market, a Western notion which has extended the trade concept to complex and enigmatic realms, has brought changes to the framework within which Indigenous art objects are made. The impact of gallery and museum on production of art works – including textile works – has meant that cultural significance has become in many cases symbolic and imbued, rather than actual, within a specific object. That is, a ceremonial belt – such as the work made by Bob Burruwal and included in the exhibition *Circles About the Body* – is not itself a ceremonial object, since it is relinquished to the market, rather than worn during ceremony; but its cultural meaning is nevertheless incorporated in the making process, through the maker's cultural location and intent. The nuances of this cultural position resonate as part of the piece, which the maker nevertheless willingly provides as an item for barter and as a work which articulates ideas and concepts in an art framework. An exchange of this particular kind would have had no framework for proceeding, in precolonial Australia. For its success as an exchange system, it requires an attitude to materiality which came with the advent and settlement of non-Indigenous cultures across the continent.

By contrast, Western paradigms for artmaking might have been hard put to come up with the explicit array of cultural complexity to be explored in Australian Indigenous work, and to grapple so candidly with the interface between conceptual and cultural/ceremonial frameworks. In the context of contemporary art practice, this interface has been confrontational in many ways, in its blurring of issues which would be much more comfortably left with their edges hard and cutting. My contention is that contemporary art in Australia has been radicalised – not by ever sharper and more conceptual honing of individual thought and expression, but by the necessity to include what could be regarded as an inimical approach, within that framework. Textile artists of various persuasions have been part of the transformative process which is undoubtedly occurring in the visual arts, but Indigenous artists in Australia have played a catalytic and central role in extending parameters which may have been regarded as fully extended. That is, boundaries had been drawn (despite Western cultural attachment to the notion of pushing boundaries), which excluded the central impetus for much Indigenous work – the cultural or ceremonial content, and the ability to permit the existence of these frameworks concurrently with others such as marketability, the exploration of ideas and a certain mobility of materiality and medium. The boundaries are now billowing nicely, assisted by the work of Indigenous textile artists in diverse and unexpected ways.

Acknowledgment
Thanks go to Jenni Dudley and Margie West for their information.

Notes

1. Louise Hamby and Doreen Mellor, 'Fibre Tracks', *Oxford Companion to Aboriginal Art and Culture* (ed. Sylvia Kleinert and Margo Neale), Oxford University Press, Melbourne, 1999.
2. Doreen Mellor, 'Exploring the dynamics of surface and origin: Australian Indigenous textile and fibre practice', *Origins and New Perspectives – Contemporary Australian Textiles* (ed. Glenda King), ex. cat., Queen Victoria Museum and Art Gallery and Craft Australia, Launceston, Tasmania, 1998.
3. Steve Hemming, 'Aboriginal Coiled Basketry in South Australia', *Journal of the Anthropological Society of South Australia*, July 1989, pp. 48–50.
4. Information collated with the assistance of Jenni Dudley, Ernabella Arts.
5. Anne Brody, *Utopia A Picture Story*, ex. cat., Tandanya National Aboriginal Cultural Institute, Adelaide, 1989.
6. Information provided by Margie West, Museum and Art Gallery of the Northern Territory.
7. Christoper Menz, *Objects from the Dreaming*, ex. cat., Art Gallery of South Australia, Adelaide, 1996, p. 3.

LIVING CULTURAL TRADITIONS: CREATIVE EXPRESSIONS OF INDIA'S POSTCOLONIAL PERIOD

Jasleen Dhamija

In 1998 India celebrated 50 years of independence. Since then, seminars, lectures and exhibitions have marked the event, but the result has been a sense of disenchantment with what is felt to be the impoverished state of India's art scene. It has been labelled intellectually impoverished, corrupt and imitative. Many practising artists have reflected much of this uncertainty and lack of confidence in their work.

Our cultural heritage consists mainly of folk and tribal art forms. This creativity reflects not only the psyche of the people, but the social, economic and political situations as well. However, before going further, it is necessary to define what we mean by folk art and craft.

I understand folk forms primarily as an expression of the day-to-day life of a community of the rituals surrounding rites of passage and a celebration of domestic rhythms. These rituals are an important part of the life of the community and all forms of creative expression, such as sculpting, painting, building, dance and song, are included in its performance. Though these artists appear anonymous, within the community they are talented individuals, known for their creativity. They in turn add to the development of the genre by adding their own vision or interpretation; however, the true motivation and inspiration comes from the community. There is a tendency among art historians to see tradition as that which is fixed and unchanging. Perhaps we should like to keep it that way, but a dynamic community is in constant change and so, consequently, are its creative expressions.

However, attitudes are changing and researchers realise that tradition is not opposed to innovation. A living cultural expression is constantly evolving.

Commercial crafts employ a large number of people. Most of these work in textiles as weavers, spinners, dyers, printers, specialised washers of fabrics, and embroiderers. In fact, after agriculture, textile production employs the greatest number of people in India and large communities are concentrated in special areas. These weavers, mostly the latest in a generation of weavers, draw inspiration from their deities, their shrines, their literature, their own oral historians, genealogists, their progenitors and even their sects and priests. It is in this context that we have to look at the art and craft scene in India. Folk art and tribal tradition did not extend into urban areas during the occupation. The colonial influences had their impact on the art world through art colleges, and on crafts, which were recognised as commercial commodities.

But during this period, the national movement encouraged traditional creativity as an expression of national identity. Karamchand Gandhi used craft production as a finely honed political weapon.

First came the call to Swadeshi to use national products and boycott the industrial produce of the colonialists, so focusing attention on the producers of handicrafts and handlooms. Gandhi made the hand-spun, hand-woven cloth, *khadi*, the political cloth for independence. Men, women and children gave up the imported machine-made cloths and in a dramatic gesture burnt them and took to wearing *khadi*. It became a major issue on the political and economic agenda, for the cottage industry was then, as now, the second largest employer after agriculture. With this legacy, the newly-formed government set up the development of crafts as an economic priority and the weavers of fabric formed the largest group in production in the non-formal sector.

The *khadi* cloth, however, became linked with Gandhi's movement of Khadi, evolving into an untouchable sacred cow. The movement, now an effective political force in the fight for independence, became close- ended and the concepts of simplicity and frugality became associated with middle-class soul-destroying bad taste.

In the rural areas the influences were filtered through the people's consciousness. They saw the changes and incorporated them. The train became an important leitmotif and defined the parameters of their life. It was absorbed into their embroideries, the painted murals in their homes. The new way of life was metaphorphiosed into new commodities – the ceiling fans, light bulbs etc. The tea pot and tea cups were woven into the bridal *durrees*, the tapestry woven *gelims*, and seemed to acquire a life of their own. The wall clock was woven into a rhythmic *ikat* pattern along with the aeroplane, symbolising the passage of time. Export markets were impressed, not only by the virtuosity of the weavers, but also by the fact that their products were highly treasured and considered an important item in their own community.

House in Orissa, India, with pattern worked by hand using rice paste on the mud walls and floor to celebrate the rice harvest.

The Story of the Maithali

The story of the Maithali paintings, known today as Madhubani painting, is an illuminating episode in our art history. The Maithali paintings were a part of the ritual life of Northern Bihar. They were discovered by a former colonial official William Archer, who later became an art historian. While posted in North Bihar, Archer was carrying out relief work after a devastating earthquake in the 1940s. He saw houses which had been torn apart, and they revealed the most extraordinary paintings on the inner walls. The very womb of the house revealed its secrets, the Kobhar *ghar*, where the newly married couple came together, surrounded by richly painted walls. These were the work of the women of the household, blessing the union of the couple. They painted the rounded benign countenance of the mother goddess. They painted the Kayakalapa. They showed the divine couples Shiva and Parvati, Radha and Krishna, and illustrations of the love act for the uninitiated. They even painted droll images of the shrewish wife and the antics of the animal kingdom. It was probably the first time that a man other than the bridegroom had seen these paintings. Archer recorded this experience and photographed it. These records became a part of the information collected by the British officials, which eventually appeared in gazetteers or in their personal memoirs.

Later in the 1960s a flood focused attention on the area and the government agencies decided to develop this art form into a product. In the process it lost the ritualistic aspect and became a commodity, but it also became known to the outside world as a rich repertoire of the folk traditions of Northern Bihar. The Maithali style of painting became known the world over as Madhubani.

Madhubani is an interesting, partially positive, illustration of what happens when this creative expression of a people is taken up for development as a product. The women were asked to paint on paper. Though they took to it with great hesitation, it freed them from the constraint of working on it only on specified occasions and within the confines of their home. Their work brought them in contact with the outside world and their horizons widened. They broke out of the confines of their traditional repertoire and incorporated images from their inner and outer world. It also suddenly became a means of earning an income and they vied with one another to produce finer and better work. Later they painted on cloth, produced silk *sarees* and dresses for the fashion world, made greeting cards and place mats, indiscriminately. It was inevitable that the distinctive styles of painting of the Kayasth and the Brahmin communities were lost.

Today everyone paints commercially, men, women and children; before it was only the mature women who painted. Although there is no doubt it has brought prosperity to a few people of the villages, unfortunately most of the paintings on sale are of very poor quality. The overall standard of painting has deteriorated considerably. Despite this situation, a few creative artists have emerged. They have gone beyond the stereotype of the traditional painting and given a new dimension to this art form. The National Crafts Museum in New Delhi has presented their work, and continues to encourage and promote them. Gangadevi is one painter with a vision to crystallise the new experiences into her traditional style and reveal her perceptions through the known symbols, whose contributions can be seen in context with the contemporary art scene. Besides her, artists Sita Devi and Jagadama Devi also rose to prominence. Except at the Crafts Museum, however, they have only been sporadically exhibited. The National Art Gallery, which presents contemporary Indian artists, has never exhibited their work. They do not command the same prices as the painters who have emerged from the art colleges. People continue to look at this particular genre of art as folkloric and thus not of intrinsic value as a form of creative expression! It is interesting that recognition of the artists has come from outside: it is in Japan that there is a Museum of Madhubani paintings.

There was an illustrative episode when John Irwin, Curator of the Indian Section at The Victoria and Albert Museum in London in the 1960s, sent us a stack of photographs of *sujanis* (embroided quilts) from the Maithali area. The *sujanis* were embroided with simplified drawings in the Maithali style. Irwin enquired if these could be copies of Paul Klee's drawings worked into 'primitive' embroidered quilts by a clever dealer. We were all very amused and identified them as authentic *sujanis* of North Bihar, worked with highly stylised drawings of the Maithali tradition of wall painting.

The process of revival and creation of a market for Madhubani paintings has not only blurred the stylistic schools, but also submerged the other traditions of area. The extraordinary terracottas made by the women for different festivals are now hardly to be seen. The highly developed abstract forms, created in the quilting technique and applique, as well as the sculpturesque forms created with golden grass, have been more or less lost. One wonders why the resurgence in one creative field should not have strengthened other areas of creativity!

In the 1950s, when India emerged from the colonial rule, we inherited a multi-layered situation in the world of creativity. There was, on the one hand, an Anglicised educated class of Indians who ran the administration, industry and educational institutions and carried out the planning of socio-cultural programmes as well as economic programmes. They looked to the West for guidance. We had inherited the arts and crafts colleges set up under the colonial system. In these colleges, Indian art was looked at as essentially prehistoric, and Indian thought was understood not as philosophy but as ethics or religious thought. During the colonial period, art history began with the Greeks. The senior artists, who went to art school before the independence of the country, even today talk of the situation in colonial terms. 'There was hardly any sculpture, except for a few plaster casts and equestrian statue.' When asked about Indian traditional art form, they are dismissive: 'Oh yes, there were a few traditional craftsmen working in marble mines at Makrana.' There was amazing disregard for the traditional *sthapathis*, who were trained in a rigorous school of architecture and sculpture. Had the art schools incorporated these traditions in the mainstream of art teaching even after independence, we would today have had a richer creative milieu.

In the area of hand-woven textiles and crafts, however, a strong movement was developed and an incredible resurgence of crafts was effectively orchestrated under the leadership of Kamaladevi Chattopadhyay. The mid-1950s and 1960s saw an active movement of revival of traditional art forms. Unfortunately, we did not distinguish between the crafts made for everyday life, which too had a deep significance in our lives, from those which were made by the men and women as a part of ritual performance and as a form of their creative expression. Everything was taken up for revival and for marketing. The urban influences began to penetrate the rural areas. The advisors, the administrators, the artists and the designers brought their attitudes, patronising the peasants, the crafts and the tribal people, who they felt needed to be helped to commercialise their skills. We inherited not only the colonial institutions of arts and cafts schools, but also the attitudes. A number of crafts were revived and remarkable work was done throughout the country. However, the creativity of the craftspersons, never really blossomed: they became experts in the techniques and in the handling of materials, but they were given the designs by the designers, who could not understand the strength or the limitation of the materials and the techniques. The rift between the master craftsman and the designers created by the art schools widened.

In some cases there were successes. For instance in the case of Kalamkari, the hand-painted and dyed fabrics, which had been virtually lost, were revived and hundreds of painters emerged as excellent creative craftsmen. This success was possibly because of Kora Ramamoorty, a painter and a collector, who was entrusted the task of reviving this art form. He learnt the techniques and painted portraits and landscapes. Today some artists are using it as a creative medium and have developed a distinct style of their own.

The master casters of Dhokra of Bastar, however, were in danger of losing their creativity when they began producing for an export market in quantity and were forced to sell their works by the kilogram. They even lost part of their local market and some of them lost their regular clientele and became alienated from their own society. The same was the fate of the creative expression of women in their embroideries. Hand-worked embroideries made for the family, from Punjab, Haryana, Bihar, Bengal, Gujarat or Karnatakata, had been a most extraordinary form of the creative expressions of the women. They were the repository not only of the family history, but also of the cultural life of the people. However, commercialisation saw the end of many of these traditions.

There has been interferenc both from the government, with unqualified designers and marketing experts of the international market, and the voluntary sector has also entered into the field since the 1980s. An exhibition organised in 1997 by the government agencies dealing with voluntary organisation showed the outreach of this movement. It also showed the total lack of sensitivity of the organisers, whose limitations were very visible in the type of product they had developed for marketing. In 1998 the Asia Society in New York organised an exhibition of quilts from Bihar, which were being produced by a voluntary organisation working amongst the women in Bihar. Their products were neither genuine, nor creative. Initially, a Ford Foundation grant had been given to the organisation for work in the field amongst women because it was doing good social work. Later a grant to The Asia Society, New York, was given to promote the quilts being produced by the women. The Asia Society brought in an advisor, who had neither knowledge of the culture of the area or the traditional folk arts, nor the time to work with the organisation in the field. She only looked at what was being produced and ordered the material for an exhibition as one would order for a shop.

It was an uninspired exhibit and it got the treatment it deserved. Few caught sight of the exhibition, which was badly displayed tucked into the basement. An opportunity for the women of North Bihar to be recognised as creative artists in the New York art world was lost.

The colonial mind-set of the cultural and educational policymakers still haunts our approach to the nurturing of the creativity of our people. No attempt has been made to include the traditional systems of education. The Schools of Architecture and Design do not have the teaching of *shilip shastras*, the old treatises of craft education or the training practices of the master builders. No attempt has been made to employ masters of these creative arts as a part of the faculty in teaching institutions. They are employed as technicians. Students are given 'exposure' to the arts and crafts traditions. What do we mean by exposure? In a country of nearly a billion people, where 75% of the people live in the rural context, where homes are built by the people without architects, and interiors and commodities are created without designers, what is the role of the designers and architects, whose education alienates them from their culture?

We continue to perpetuate the mistakes of the past by interfering with the creativity of the craftsmen and women, who are skilled in the handling of the materials and tools, and have a well-honed ability to recognise the needs of their society and look at their work in the light of their education and ex-perience. For them it is a part of their *dharma*, and the very act of creation is a form of prayer. For example, the felt-making Mansooris of Kutch, who are Sufis, create the felt through multiple rhythms as they call upon the name of Hazrat Ali. For them the creation is a form of *zikr*, as it is a form of *jap* for the noviates of the Kanphata sect, who embroider the sacred bag for their guru. I remember vividly the response I got from one young noviate, who sat absorbed in the embroidery of a bag. I asked him, like a good researcher, what did he call the pattern and he replied 'Jhopu Jhopu'. 'What does it mean?' I asked; and he only laughed, but his companion said, 'That is his name'! He was creating his offering, his space, in the world of his guru.

The master designer-weaver M. Jafar Ali Nakshabandi and his father before him, Ali Hasan of Varanasi, made the *jala*, the *naksha*, the traditional jacquard with extraordinary skill and sensitivity. Their entire life was devoted to the principles of their Pir, Bahaudin-Naqshabandi, the head of the great Sufi sect. They may design, weave and sell to an unknown market, yet their involvement is intense.

Unfortunately, all of us have been responsible for interfering with the delicately balanced creative world of the craftspersons. A patronising attitude still persists. We have not done anything to create an awareness of the richness of their cultural heritage. Nor have we been able to bring them into the mainstream of contemporary life. Perhaps we should examine the parallel example of performing arts, the classical traditions of music, dance and drama. How is it that we have excelled in these forms of expression? The traditional musicians, dancers and actors have come into the mainstream of society. Is it because music, dance and drama are part of the educational system? No one makes these comparisons.

The government organisations and spokespersons are always ready to speak at international seminars and present the richness of India's cultural traditions, but none has questioned the cultural policies and asked where did our indigenous art forms fit in. No one has asked whether the policies of the 1950s are valid today. Do the old institutions of design centres, weavers' centres and technical schools and the much touted Guru-Shish Parampara, the traditional form of apprenticeship, fulfill the needs of the craft world of today? Or do they lead to child labour and denial of a normal development for the children of craftspersons? And what impact are international exhibitions and awards having on our traditions? Is the creativity of the people being stifled or is it growing? Is the economic agenda being served by the present-day policies or are we bartering with our cultural heritage?

Even today we have national and international seminars, where academics, art historians, anthropologists, interventionists or crafts facilitators and administrators read erudite papers, but without any participation of the creative individuals. We talk of the need to raise the status of the masters, but our own attitude is patronising. An international seminar held in India in 1999, entitled 'Makers and Meaning', drew a number of participants from all over the world. People were flown in not only from different parts of India, but from all over the world. However, the makers were absent and the academicians dissected the makers and extracted the meaning according to their lights.

It was in the 1980s that J. Swaminathan, a painter of repute and a person with a social conscience, as well as a questioning, questing mind, began to work with the creative people of Bastar, a district in Madhya Pradesh inhabited by a tribal people who have a rich cultural life. He had been researching folk art for nearly fifteen years. The Bharat Kala Bhawan, a cultural centre in Bhopal in central India, was an excellent base for him to work from. He raised his voice in protest against the approach of the government and also of the established art world to the folk, tribal and traditional expressions. In what way was the work of a tribal painter less than the work of a fine artist, he questioned the art world? He went ahead to hold an exhibition at the Bharat, Kala Bhawan, where the work of the tribal artists hung alongside that of the contemporary artist. He organised workshops where the painters and sculptors from art schools worked together with the tribal masters in an exciting print-making workshop.

Earlier, Shankho Chowdary, a sculptor, had also begun to create an awareness of the tribal and folk art amongst his students in the School of Arts at Baroda. A talented painter and researcher, Haku Shah emerged from this group to make a remarkable contribution to the study of crafts and the nurturing of the talent of creative craftspersons. He was able not only to research and focus on the nature of the folk and tribal expression, but also to encourage the development of artists such as Saroja Behn who created large applique hangings which were shown by a private gallery in Philadelphia, and Gopal, an itinerant bard who transferred his melodic song to line drawings on paper. However, it is Swaminathan who has had an impact on the art world and who has also created an awareness amongst the practitioners of traditional art, possibly because he had the backing of an institution, the Bharat Kala Bhawan.

The recent exhibition put up by Dr Jyotindra Jain, Director of the National Handloom and Handicrafts Museum, entitled *Other Masters* (1998–9) reiterates the same message. The exhibition presented the work of five contemporary folk and tribal artists and was a moving experience. Sonabai, a simple middle-aged village woman from a backward village of Central Asia, had recreated her own world in an installation of mud walls, textured with the movement of the fingers, with raised patterns and sculpted forms. Seated figures looked out of the shrine with a look of wonderment at the world. When questioned about her work and her inspiration, Sonabai just gestured gently to her work. 'It is all there,' she said.

Neelamani Devi, with her refined features and her long *vaishnav* sandalwood mark on her forehead, had her extraordinary pots on display. She builds her pots without the use of a wheel and each form appears monumental and fits in with the quote from fifteenth-century writer Abdul-er Razak: 'the sun, the moon and the rains have brought them to perfection'.

Jangarh Singh Shyam, a shy young man, who used to help his mother to recreate and paint their village, found himself in the friendly environs of the studios of Bharat Kala Bhawan. Today he is a powerful painter and the mythical and mundane develop a life of their own as he paints on the walls or on his canvas. His goddesses, the soaring birds and the leaping tiger are always in motion and their eyes have a look of wonder as though each one of them is looking out of Jangarh's eyes at this amazing new world.

Jivya Soma Mashe, a painter from Warli, recreated his world with infinite patience and sense of mystery. He is untouched by the glitterati moving around him, be they in Delhi Bombay, Tokyo or New York.

The fifth painter, Ganga Devi, is no longer with us. Her large painting 'Cycle of Life' dominates, painted with a freshness of vision seeking for a new vocabulary of expression, while still using the ritual conventional forms. A woman, who is pregnant, stands in a mango grove surrounded by birds and fruits. The child appears ready to enter the world. She plucks a ripe mango as she looks with her large eyes at the world around her. Devi's 'Cancer Ward' series is an extraordinary expression of this strange world into which she has entered.

These are important events in our cultural history. But will they have a lasting and widespread effect to create an awareness and change in government policy? Will the national institutions for promoting contemporary art – Lalit Kala Academy, the National Museum of Modern Art, the art galleries – open their doors for the creative artists who are not from the elite background of the painters, sculptors and fabric artists of today? What of the art critics in India, with their rather esoteric writing, which is imitative in style and content and which is more interested in demonstrating their knowledge of the work of art critics in the West than in the work under review? Will they be able to look at tribal and folk art as an art form in its own right?

Today the contemporary art scene is obsessed with installations. They are talked of as a new form of expression. Strangely enough every festival, every temple, shrine and home has an installation. Installation is a way of life in a traditional society. The extraordinary installations for the worship of Bhadrakali are formed by the recreation of the shrine by the priest who uses effectively all the materials available to him to create the presence of the goddess. This is a most evocative piece of art. Why did we have to discover installation only when it became the rage in the West, whose artists created a world of magic in the barren landscape of their dying civilisation?

I am reminded of a lesson I was taught by a metalsmith in Isphahan, Iran. I asked him how he knew that his apprentice was working well, when he was sitting outside drinking tea with his friends, and he responded, 'From the rhythm of his hammer strokes!' He laughed at me and, singing the rhythmic pattern of the strokes, said, 'When he makes a mistake it is the disruption of that rhythm which I catch'.

Perhaps some lessons could be learnt from the experience of other countries. The Australian policy of nurturing the Aboriginal art might be a good example to study. The experiment carried out by David Williams at the Canberra School of Arts of holding a print-making workshop with the Aboriginal artists and then absorbing some of the students into the School has resulted in the creation of a very strong print-making department. Amongst Australian Indigenous communities, the introduction of skills such as Batik work from Indonesia was done with a great deal of discernment and has given rise to a distinctive school of cloth paintings.

A recent workshop organised by the Crafts Council of talented young craftspersons was synchronised with a workshop of traditional musicians. Strangely enough, it was the lack of funding that led to the synchronisation of the two workshops. The young artists shared their knowledge and an interesting, lively exchange took place. The musicians were painting and carving, and the craftspersons were singing and dancing. The resulting work was full of vitality. A young wood carver wanted to sing, to play on the *sarangi*, a stringed instrument. He dreamt of carving a *sarangi* which would be not only the most beautiful but also the most melodious. I pondered on how this had happened, and realised: Ah! It is the recreation of the atmosphere of a community celebration, where all forms of expression were brought together, which has worked this miracle.

Today we have lost touch with the actual reality; the ability to reach the inner workings of the psyche. Our self-conscious efforts, our preconceived notions have stifled our spontaneity, our joy, our ability to celebrate with abandon and express ourselves. I crave an art that passionately transcends the mundane and transports one to another world.

KAPDA

Nima Poovaya-Smith

Allowing for slight variations in spelling and pronunciation, almost all North Indian and Pakistani languages refer to cloth or clothing as *kapda*. It is a word that carries a direct, simple unadorned resonance. This is in contrast to the connotations of lavish embellishment that traditional South Asian textiles usually convey with hundreds perhaps thousands of years of expertise behind them. The Sanskrit word *vastra*, for instance, has beauty implicit in it; *kapda*, by contrast, is linked with something basic and fundamental. A number of years ago the amazing legendary film institution, Bollywood, produced a film called *Roti, Kapda aur Makhan* which translates into 'bread, clothing and shelter', the bare necessities of life. *KAPDA* is also the eponymous name of a textile project in Britain, initiated by Yorkshire and Humberside Arts, the region's principal funding and arts development body. This chapter concludes with a description of this project.

Mahatma Gandhi, in a masterly economic, political and psychological act, made *khadi*, or homespun cloth, the symbol of Indian resistance to British imperialism. *Khadi* is precisely the kind of cloth that the word *kapda* conjures up, plain and unpretentious, although today it has somewhat evolved from that humble yet potent textile that Gandhi spun. He presented a length of this fabric as a wedding gift to the then Princess Elizabeth, to the reported fury of the Queen Mother, who perceived this to be an insult. In a recent exhibition of the Queen's collections, however, the piece of cloth was displayed with due honour. In many ways this symbolises the troubled relationship Britain has had with Indian textiles. From critical admiration of the wondrous textiles to decrying them because they did not employ the superior technology of the Industrial Revolution, to banning and suppressing them in favour of much cruder British imports, Indian textiles have played a dominant role in the power struggles between the two countries. Suppression had ramifications that were far wider than the merely economic. It comprised an entire culture's identity and aesthetic sensibility as well. This is still in the process of being reclaimed.

The relationship has altered radically in post-independence, post-war Britain. The reasons for this are two-fold. Firstly, many members of the large South Asian community in Britain dress traditionally as a matter of course. Secondly, and independent of this, variations of high-street fashions have swept through Britain, from the cheap and cheerful Indian textiles of the 1960s to the more upmarket variations of the 1990s. The first phenomenon was almost without any fashion status, tolerated rather than admired and certainly seldom copied. The traditional North Indian and Pakistani costume, the *shalwar kameez*, for instance, both supremely comfortable and functional, was firmly relegated to the 'other' and viewed as rather shapeless ethnic gear. It took Jemima Khan and the late Diana, Princess of Wales to make visible a costume worn by Asian women in Britain for over 30 years. Before Jemima Khan and the Princess of Wales a few ordinary British women had worn the *shalwar kameez*, drawn by its practicality and in order to express solidarity with their Asian friends. They invariably had a dual response – warm compliments from Asian acquaintances, studied silence from their own compatriots. Jemima Khan and the Princess, however, commanded fashion credibility. Suddenly the *shalwar kameez*, or variations of it, was conferred status. Through fashion houses such as Libas, which has the luxury of its own glossy fashion magazine giving access to the South Asian communities in the Indian sub-continent, Britain and the Middle East, people began to recognise its *haute couture* potential. Tradition and trendiness were suddenly being combined.

This essay will explore, briefly, four textile projects that have taken place in Britain and which have a clearly defined relationship with the South Asian sub-continent. Of these, two were initiated by Bradford Art Galleries and Museums and toured to other regions: *101 Saris From India* (1992) and *The Draped and the Shaped: Costumes and Textiles from Pakistan* (1997). *Shamiana: Mughal Tent* was a dream skilfully transformed into reality by the late Shireen Akbar of the Victoria and Albert Museum which involved museums and galleries not just within Britain but around the world; it had its grand collective opening at the V & A in 1997. Sadly, Akbar herself was not there to witness her triumph. All three projects have had a seminal influence on the thinking behind *KAPDA*, a project undertaken in partnership with the cities of Bradford in West Yorkshire and Rotherham in South Yorkshire.

The defining context, for me, was through the first exhibition, which demonstrated clearly the strength of the links between identity and apparel. I curated the exhibition *101 Saris From India* for Bradford Art Galleries and Museums in 1992 (the title was a metaphor for the Indian practice of dealing only with odd numbers for auspicious occasions and did not actually reflect the number of saris in the exhibition, which was far higher). Bradford's cultural composition is very diverse and out of a population of just under half a million, nearly 80,000 are of South Asian descent. By 1992 Bradford had already built up a modest textile holding in order that the collections should reflect the cultures of the South Asian communities of West Yorkshire, of which Bradford is a major district. The collections included a number of embroidered dowry textiles from Gujarat in Western India, and a selection of Kanchipuram and Dharmavaram saris from South India.

A classic garment that has been in fashion for nearly 2,000 years, the sari is unstitched but highly structured, and can be worn without adaptation whether you are size 8 or 18. It seemed appropriate to introduce it to a wider world than just that of its South Asian initiates. The style of the draping today, by and large, is confined to a small number of recognisable styles although historically it has had a much wider range of styles. The exhibition included a small collection of antique saris, but the main body was devoted to special creations by master weavers reviving disappearing design motifs and weaves. The exhibition had been personally selected by Brij Bhasin, at that time Managing Director of the Handloom and the Handicraft Corporation of the Government of India. Passionate about all Indian crafts, particularly textiles, and dedicated to the notion of excellence in contemporary craft production, each sari had been hand picked, a fine blend of the historical and the contemporary, eloquently expressing regional variety and richness. Many of the saris articulated revivals of motifs and techniques that had been in decline.

Unusually for Bradford Art Galleries and Museums, apart from a small selection of saris that were on loan, this was a selling exhibition. Initially dismayed at the prospect of being responsible for merchandising such a large number of textiles, it quickly became apparent that people of all culture were responding to the textiles with a warmth and immediacy that was quite startling. And in these more or less standard lengths of silk, cotton, organza, gold and silver brocade, with their glorious scrolling motifs, foliate design, peacocks, parrots, temples, chariots, geese, tigers, lions, creatures of fantasy, railway carriages and hieratic figures of gods and goddesses, here was a veritable cornucopia. The unknown artists who conceived and distilled this lexicon of images would be considered inferior to the fine artist as we understand the term today. They do not need this endorsement because the sari has its own splendid *raison d'etre*. It is not just part of a living tradition; it is in a literal sense a vital tradition. In some ways the sari can be described as participatory sculpture that needs the human figure for its multiple meanings to come alive. A flat, defined length of cloth, usually patterned with motifs that range from arcane religious references to the bounteousness of the natural world, is given form and a three-dimensional presence by the wearer. If a woman so chooses, she can convey a number of messages through her choice of sari, her marital status, her area of origin and even her caste.

It was obvious that a number of the saris were perfect additions to the Bradford collection. They combined beauty with timelessness. They also represented expertise of surface decoration and weaving. Their contemporaneity

Sari, Varanasi, India (19th century)
brocaded silk
510 x 114.5cm
collection of Bradford Art Galleries & Museums

underlined the identity of large groups of Asians within West Yorkshire. In one way or another, all groups related to the sari, and even if not universally worn, it was widely understood.

Curators can be ruthless and crafty. I swiftly identified the saris I wanted for the collection, sorted out the duplicates and made those available to the public for sale. To our amazement, the buyers were Asian and British, men and women. To be sure, the non-traditional buyers were usually buying in order to display, but the primary reason was enjoyment. The expression on the faces of South Asian women when they are eyeing saris with a view to buying is fascinating. As they make up their minds, the expressions change from the tentative to the cool, collected and very determined. Needless to say, the saris sold briskly. The acquisition of over one hundred saris from the exhibition not only provided the Bradford textile collections with critical mass, but the sales to the public highlighted the stubbornness and loyalty with which people had clung to a costume which, on the surface, was not the most practical. However, any formal or celebratory function is marked by its proud presence. This guarantees that the buying of it and therefore the patronage of an ancient craft continues to be vigorous.

The design of the exhibition was crucial to its success with the public. (Its audience was not confined to the Bradford public, since *101 Saris* toured to nearly a dozen other venues around the country.) The design brief was specific about wanting a display that allowed for the sophisticated analysis as well as pleasure of the exhibition rather than the reinforcing of stereotypes of the sub-continent. Terry Brown, the exhibition designer, demonstrated both drama and subtlety in his concept. A number of cool white-on-white cotton and pale pastel saris from Chanderi and Maheshwari in Madhya Pradesh and Venkatgiri in Andhra Pradesh were stretched on frames and placed in front of the shuttered windows, acting as mock window screens. They acted as a contrapuntal device to the opalescent colours that abounded elsewhere in the gallery. Saris, representing the colours of the rainbow, were wound round a central axis sited on a wide circular plinth, where one set of borders was arranged in a stylised swirl, with the opposite set of borders splaying out above from a tall copper urn at full stretch to create a canopy. A loom-like structure displayed *ikats*, brocades and a range of other saris patterned at the loom. This included a particularly striking piece of Orissa *ikat*. At an end corner of the gallery, temple saris from Kanchipuram and Dharmavaram were draped in a structured cascade, forming an architectural pattern very like the *ziggurat* temple motifs of their borders. The designer was trying to emulate the busy design of South Indian temples. This was further reinforced by surmounting the structure with a large majestic image of the elephant-headed god Ganesh. Appropriately, this was a gift from the Government of India to the Gallery. As the Remover of all Obstacles, Ganesh is regarded as one of the most auspicious and benevolent of gods within the Hindu pantheon and he is regularly invoked at marriage and house-warming ceremonies.

Mannequins made of wood and cord were decked out in saris in different regional styles. Members of the Asian community helped the Gallery with the intricacies of draping them in the Bengali style and the Maharashtrian style. The latter required nine yards rather than the regulation six yards and involved tucking the sari between the legs rather like a pair of pantaloons. There was even an abbreviated mini style from the tribal regions of Madhya Pradesh. Anxious to appear accessible without rendering the saris vulnerable to curious and irresistible handling, cordon ropes were put up. These were wound round with old silk and cotton saris donated by members of the community, so people could still have a tactile sense of the exhibition without damaging the actual exhibits. Saris were stacked in orderly piles in a mock-up of a shop; vegetable-dyed cottons were twined from tree branches and one even emerged serpent-like from a large cane basket. It was opulence and restraint at the same time. The saris had been treated with the profound respect they deserved, yet their richness had not been quelled or deadened in any way.

In the face of such overwhelming beauty, modernity can appear to be an impertinence. We decided to take a risk and commission three British-based textile artists to produce a sari apiece. As an intellectual and experimental exercise alone, the commissions were interesting. Fahmida Shah and Sarbjit Natt use textiles as a canvas on which to print and paint produced saris in sumptuous silk and tissue respectively, characterised by their very personal design vocabularies. Shah's expressionist exuberance contained architectural references, whereas Natt's much more structured designs were drawn directly from the embroidery traditions of her native Punjab. In the Punjabi *phulkaris* and *baghs*, the geometric and the curvilinear were ingeniously combined by women embroiderers to depict belief systems and world views that were often quite modern. The third textile artist, Anita Sheshan, is actually a weaver and wove a sari in such heavy silk that many of the members of the public thought it was wool, yet it draped with the supple fluidity of the lightest of silks. Unconsciously or atavistically, she had chosen colours, jade green with turquoise blue borders, that recalled the richness of the temple saris of South India, her father's area of origin.

The nature of the crafts practised by these three women, British through citizenship and Asian through descent, has sufficient anomalies with the manner in which crafts are practised within the Indo-Pakistan sub-continent to make it worhty of comment. A Crafts Council survey conducted a few years ago found that there were approximately 25,000 practising craftspeople in England, Scotland and Wales. Of these, only 1.2% are of minority descent and this includes people of African, Afro-Caribbean, Chinese, Indian, Pakistani and Bangladeshi origin. And out of these groups, people from the Indian subcontinent constitute, in percentage terms, the smallest number. There are both historical and contemporary reasons for this paucity in numbers. But what is quite clear is that a question of status, or lack of it, has not only restricted the numbers of makers of minority descent, but has also affected the crafts in general in Britain in crucial areas of its infrastructure – mainly funding, exhibiting and training. It is difficult to come up with more than 15–20 recognised names of makers of South Asian descent who practise their craft on a professional basis. But while the numbers are low, the quality of the work of this small group is exceptionally high. A number of the makers are developing an international reputation and have their work in public collections. If the quality of the work is so high, why are the numbers so low? The answer to this question involves not only a critique of the contemporary milieu in Britain, but also the status accorded to crafts both in Britain and the Indian sub-continent within a historical context.

It would be appropriate, at this point, to make a comparative reference to the fine arts. The hierarchical distinction between the fine arts and the crafts has impacted on the crafts in a manner that has been distinctly to its disadvantage. There are a far higher number of painters, printmakers and sculptors of South Asian descent than there are makers and this situation, according to anecdotal evidence, appears to be manifested in student numbers as well as in the relevant courses. The fact that most makers in this country tend to enrol when they are aged around 30 may have a bearing on this. Indeed, a surprising number of people turn to the crafts when they have turned 40. But in the case of South Asian makers, the reason for this discrepancy has its roots in the attitude towards crafts in the Indian sub-continent.

Many of the established fine artists now living and working in Britain grew up in the sub-continent and had their initial training there. Anish Kapoor, Dhruva Mistry, Saleem Arif, Avtarjeet Dhanjal, Ali Zaidi and Tehmina Shah are a few examples of this. While they may not necessarily have acted as role models, their numbers were swollen by a group of artists, usually younger, who had grown up in Britain, for instance, Sutapa Biswas, Gurminder Sikand, Perminder Kaur and Zarina Bhimji. The 1980s saw them emerge, if not as a cohesive group (although some art galleries did try and treat them as an automatically homogeneous unit) at least as a politicised one. There were exceptions to this. Anish Kapoor's phenomenal success seemed to place him in a category of his own. And although since the late 1980s, in particular, these artists have made a determined effort not to be marginalised, there is still a common ground that goes beyond shared ethnicity, even if this common ground is no more than a shared concern to be treated as part of the general mainstream.

There has not been a parallel movement within the crafts. Nor has there been a similar movement of craftspeople from the sub-continent to this country. The reason is tied up with status. Crafts in the sub-continent still tends to be a hereditary or caste-based occupation. The periodic waves of people from the sub-continent to Britain usually involved individuals and families from farming, carpenter and cobbler communities, with a thin sprinkling of professional people such a doctors and engineers. None of them came here to continue their caste or hereditary occupations, but usually to work within industry.

No craftspeople appear to have emigrated to Britain in the way fine artists did. 'Appear' is used advisedly because there is possibly a sad tale of loss implicit in this. A few years ago I was approached by a frail, elderly Pakistani gentleman in Bradford. He spoke with lucidity, passion and conviction. He maintained that a number of early Asian settlers to Bradford had been hereditary craftsmen – primarily goldsmiths, weavers and potters. However, they had come here to earn a living and there was no market for their skills. They disappeared into the maws of the dark, satanic mills. My informant said he had a dream – to seek out these craftsmen, many of them perhaps living in retirement, and to provide them with the opportunity to resurrect their skills. As the years pass, that hope must recede, but *KAPDA* has been partly prompted by elements of this dream.

Artists from the sub-continent came to Britain with every intention of continuing as artists. If there were craftspeople who came too, they lacked this confidence. The arts, very early on in India, became entwined with a reconnection with one's cultural roots and with nationalism. It also tended to draw its practitioners from a relatively privileged and literate class. The aristocratic Raja Ravi Varma of Trivandrum and members from the illustrious Tagore family including Rabindranath Tagore himself are examples. It moved through a well-charted path of nostalgic revivalism and aggressive nationalism to a increasingly confident, idiomatic and personal language. This is particularly embodied in the works of artists such as Jamini Roy and Amrita Sher-Gil.

The crafts were also invoked during the freedoom struggle; in fact they managed to become its central symbol. But the person who invoked them was no hereditary or caste craftsman, he was a lawyer turned savant. Gandhi was passionate in his espousal of homespun cloth which he spun himself, using a traditional spinning wheel. That wheel is now on the national flag of

India, but perhaps the crafts have fared better as a symbol than in reality. In fact it seems to have moved through a repetitious cycle of part revival and decline. In the sub-continent today, the crafts continue to provide full-time employment for millions of people, but for many of them the income they earn is little more than a pittance – although their work is an increasingly important source of foreign exchange. The quality of the work is varied, but there are still staggeringly beautiful pieces being produced. There have been exquisite revivals and intelligent adaptations of tradition.

Outside the caste occupation structure, today, there are a number of studio potters and textile designers. But they seem more allied with the world of commercial interior design and fashion than with art. If this is doing them an injustice, it is because they do not have the same outlets of publications and exhibitions as artists do and that in itself is telling. There are excellent colleges of design in Baroda and Delhi but their intake of students is still tiny. The National College of Art in Lahore actually has a course on pottery but finds it difficult to attract students, since it is associated with a lowly hereditary trade. In spite of some enlightened patronage, the crafts have yet to achieve the status of the fine arts. This, of course, mirrors the situation in the West. While it may not operate along such harsh, demarcatory lines, it can operate in more invidious ways. This is reflected in the relatively low public funding the crafts attract in comparison with the arts. The irony about artists such as Fahmida Shah, Aneeta Sheshan and Sarbjit Natt [see colour plates 4 and 5] is that, had they lived in their countries of cultural origin, they probably would not have pursued these particular craft occupations. To that extent, their expatriate status has allowed them to operate outside the constraints of caste or hereditary occupation. This is particularly true in the case of the weaver Aneeta Sheshan. It is also the start of imbuing the crafts with the status it still lacks in the South Asian sub-continent as, inevitably, more people of South Asian descent begin to practise a variety of crafts.

The purchase of a large collection of saris from *101 Saris* transformed the collection. However, it also highlighted a glaring absence. The majority of the South Asian population of Bradford were Muslims from Pakistan. Among the Pakistani and Sikh communities of Bradford, the *shalwar kameez* takes precedence over the sari, although Muslims in both India and Pakistan wear saris. A long tunic worn with loose trousers with a large shawl-like scarf, and associated with the North of the sub-continent, the *shalwar kameez* has achieved something no other costume has managed to achieve in the sub-continent. It has not so much dislodged the sari as complemented it. It is widely regarded as an alternative costume and even traditionalists wear it without feeling they are being rebellious. Today the *shalwar kameez* can lay as much claim asthe sari to being a national costume. Bollywood and Pakistani cinema still exert a powerful influence on younger-generation Asians in Britain and since actresses frequently wear the *shalwar kameez*, cinema has provided an additional impetus. In Britain its practical advantages over the sari are obvious. Clever adaptations make it even more user-friendly without sacrificing integrity or original design. For the British Asian woman, its pervasiveness and increasing stylishness must be a cause for pleasure, as for once fashion and practicality can go hand in hand.

It was obvious that the collections and the exhibition programme needed to reflect this. *The Draped and the Shaped: Costumes and Textiles of Pakistan* was a serendipitous happening. On a visit to Lahore in order to finalise an exhibition on contemporary art by Pakistani women artists entitled *An Intelligent Rebellion* (1994), I was invited by Sehyr Saigol, the managing editor of *Libas*, to discuss at her home a feature-length article on the exhibition. In the course of the conversation, she showed me some of the outfits she had designed for a fashion show in the Middle East. There were a whole range of fine white voile and cotton *shalwar kameezes* embroidered in the Lucknowi *chikkankari* technique. This was white-on-white work, using a repertoire of over thirty stitches or *tankas*. It was immediately obvious that these elegant creations were quite unlike anything I had seen before. There was a sophistication to the tailoring and an attention to detail, such as the crocheted buttons, and the hems and seams done by hand, that gave the ensembles confident claim to haute couture status. Saigol invited me to her airy workshops the following day to look at other creations her team of women embroiderers and tailors had wrought so wonderfully. Some of these costumes formed the nucleus of a collection for Bradford which was added to in subsequent years and included other designers such as Noor Jehan Bilgrami.

The Draped and the Shaped drew from a number of sources and included costumes and lengths of unstitched textiles such as wall hangings and shawls. Bradford already had a tiny, historical collection of turbans, caps, sashes, *kurtas* and *Quran* bags from different regions of Pakistan. Coupled with private loans of *phulkaris*, *khes* and *ajrakhs*, they created a context and reference point for the contemporary costumes, primarily designed by Sehyr Saigol and Noor Jehan Bilgrami. Yet there are a number of idiosyncratic similarities between the historical and the contemporary. The contemporary costumes, although perhaps tailored and styled differently from the historical textiles, had clearly intertwined surface decoration and woven patterns. The close, often lavishly worked surfaces are a common feature of all the textiles.

If *101 Saris* worked as one kind of signifier by allowing outsiders access to its complexities and simplicities (designs that need incredible skill for a costume that needs absolutely no tailoring), *The Draped and the Shaped* provided another kind of signifier. Western visitors to the exhibition were able to view at close range a dazzling range of exotic fabrics; they also saw the craftsmanship involved not just in the creation of the fabrics but also in their tailoring. The finish was of a quality that challenged and overthrew the notion of the Indo-Pakistan sub-continent as a source of cheap labour for the manufacture of garments for the high street designers in the West. Jemima Khan and the Princess of Wales notwithstanding, this was the first time one felt the convergence of the two worlds: the seemingly closed world of the Asian women wearing a traditional costume which usually marked her out for racist attention at worst or cool neutrality at best; and the world of fashion and rapidly changing trends where costumes from other cultures did not get a look in. A number of high-minded Western women tell me that they disapprove of their compatriots wearing Eastern clothes because it smacks of cultural appropriation. When I raise the question of Asian women wearing Western clothes and whether that is appropriation, the response invariably 'Oh, that's different'. Setting aside this admirable sensitivity about cultural approprialion, how about cultural appreciation? You find the clothes so overwhelmingly beautiful that you just want to wear them.

The Draped and the Shaped (which then toured the country) had been preceded by another textile event, the ramifications of which are still felt by small groups of women all over Britain and is yet to be properly assessed. A national, indeed international, project, *Shamiana: The Mughal Tent*, was seminal in the nature of its multi-layered engagements. The word *Shamiana* itself is a Persian/Urdu word meaning a large tent, usually set up for a celebratory event such as a wedding. The tent involved over fifty richly decorated panels, devised and produced by groups of mainly South Asian women and girls from around the UK and other parts of the world. The works were displayed in a number of galleries, in all their splendour.

Initiated by the Victoria and Albert Museum, home to one of the best South Asian collections in the world, the project had a number of regional partners, but for the V&A in particular it was the coming together of a number of things. Disenfranchised Asian women were setting foot inside the V&A for the first time. There was a direct sustained encounter with their own creativity, which took many women by excited surprise. The collective exploration of this creativity was within a structured space and time-frame. They were in immediate contact with the creativity of the past, produced by men and women with whom there was a direct cultural link. There were multiple interactions – within the group, with the artist tutors, with other museum staff mediated through Shireen and the museum collection itself.

Shireen had initially visited the groups and through illustrated talks about the museum and the collections familiarised them with an institution that could otherwise have appeared intimidating.

Similar yet different dynamics were taking place in other parts of the country and the world. As it continues to tour, *Shamiana*, like its architect Shireen, leaves an indelible impression. The leaflet that accompanies this exhibition describes the alienation that South Asian women of all generations can feel. South Asian women are often responsible for the maintenance of a life still centred on the home, the family and the temple, mosque or Gurudwara. Living in areas of high unemployment in the inner cities, many are forced to supplement the meagre income of their extended families by taking in piecework for the garment industry. The older generation are conscious of disinterest, even hostility, towards their cultural and religious practices, and the younger generation feel excluded from the youth culture of Britain.

The *qanats* or decorated textile panels which decked opulent Mughal and Rajput tented encampments might inspire those who were themselves skilled both in contemporary machine textile techniques and in traditional hand methods of sewing and embroidery. But, just as importantly, the image of the tent would signify the uncertainty and danger faced by migrants and refugees, experiences which were part of the life histories of many of the first participants.

Many of the British groups that joined the project in its second phase consisted of women of diverse backgrounds. Punjabi found herself next to Bengali, Bengali next to Gujarati. 'I never thought that I, as a Hindu, would work on an Islamic thing,' said one participant. 'We were a social group with differing views, yet the finished work comes across as very coherent,' commented another. A group of non-Asian women in rural Somerset joined the project because they wanted to understand the lives of people with different backgrounds and perspectives. By 1997 over eight hundred women in nine different countries had been involved in the project.

KAPDA in many ways is a natural evolution of the three projects discussed above. As a Regional Arts Board, Yorkshire and Humberside Arts is not only a funding body, but strategically invests its funding in areas that need strengthening. This could be a particular artform, geographic sub-region, or in this instance, transculturalism. *KAPDA* is part of the drive to strengthen the nascent cultural industries' infrastructure of the South Asian community in Yorkshire. Yorkshire has a substantial South Asian population of over 2 million, mainly concentrated in West Yorkshire. It was felt that the majority of this community did not appear to benefit from current arts provision within the county. Nor did they benefit from the funding system, even though those applicants who did bid for money were usually successful. There were just not enough to create a critical mass.

101 Saris, The Draped and the Shaped and *Shamiana* demonstrated clearly that, whether functional or decorative, textiles were not only powerful expressions of identity but that traditional techniques and motifs continued to be applied to contemporary themes in a particularly vibrant manner.

There is a significant pool of skills among the South Asian women of Yorkshire in cutting, tailoring and embroidery. Judging from observed and anecdotal evidence, there is an immediacy of response to textiles in their myriad forms. As a domestic activity textiles are something women can shape, structure and decorate for their family. Along with the greatly undervalued creative act of everyday cooking it gives them a sense of worth. Frequently the skills with textiles are transformed into an economic benefit for these women. However, this activity is often far removed from pleasurable creativity. The sweatshop conditions within which they operate is nothing short of sheer drudgery.

By developing existing skills in cutting, tailoring and embroidery among South Asian women – the most disenfranchised within this community – *KAPDA* aims to provide them with access to excellence as well as provide them with business and marketing skills to make their skills economically viable. *KAPDA* is intended to be a practical demonstration of Yorkshire and Humberside's mission statement of 'promoting creativity' within the broadest possible cultural context.

KAPDA aims to upskill potential or rudimentary ability into a much more creative, satisfying and economically rewarding field of activity. The training will involve skilled embroiderers from Britain, and if possible from the sub-continent, together with designers, cutters and tailors. The project is intended to provide the trainees with access to textile collections such as those held by Bradford and the V&A. The training is also meant to explore the use of environmentally friendly materials such as vegetable dyes as opposed to chemical dyes. As part of the process of providing access to excellence, the project will have formal links with art galleries in Yorkshire with South Asian communities such as those in Bradford and Rotherham. Initially, the project will be led by the Cultural Diversity Officers of both cities.

KAPDA is a unique project and, if successful, will provide one of the most quantifiable links between creative industries and regeneration. Part of the project's work will involve the development of links with *haute couture* fashion houses as well as high street fashion. There are quality fashion outlets within Britain for South Asian clothes, designed and produced in India and Pakistan. The prices Asian customers are prepared to pay for clothes for special occasions can be surpnsingly high. It was felt that the groups trained through *KAPDA* could offer competitive rates. It is also the intention that the targeted market will not just be Asian customers.

In its attempt to engage with cultural industries and reposition textile activity into a more creative, imaginative realm without losing its economic context, *KAPDA* should prove an interesting and hopeful experiment. Whether it will be sustainable and successful only time will tell. It might well be only a modest footnote in the epic relationship between the sub-continent and Britain in which textiles have played such a crucial role. It is not without its elements of dream. The spinners, weavers, colourists and embroiderers of the past did create wondrous and magic fabrics, either sheer and delicate, rich and lustrous, or simple and elegant. *KAPDA* is a homage to this, and also to the craftsmen who came to this country in the early years of settlement and did not even dare to dream of practising their craft because it would not have provided them with a sustainable livelihood.

I believe that creativity is the birthright of every human being.

YINKA SHONIBARE: DRESSING DOWN TEXTILES IN A VICTORIAN PHILANTHROPIST'S PARLOUR

Janis Jefferies

'I am actually producing something perceived as ethnic in inverted commas, but at the same time the African fabric used in my work is something industrially produced and, given its cultural origins, my own authenticity is questioned.' [1]

Yinka Shonibare has emerged as one of a generation of artists from the British Afro-Asian diaspora who, in the words of one writer Oguibe Olu, mimic cultural stereotypes and resist 'our' traditional perceptions of 'their' art as an 'anthropological window into an ethnic mind'. [2]

What kinds of authenticity does Shonibare question? What story is he trying to tell? Although Shonibare works in several media, since 1991 he has become known for his use of 'traditional' West African fabrics, although he is equally recognised for his decorative painting in which printed textiles replace canvas.

This essay explores Shonibare's re-importation but strategic use of 'ethnic' fabric as a means of unravelling the complex web of relationships between Europeans (significantly British) and those they colonised. Within what appears to be a deceptive patterning of familiar visual and tactile idioms, Shonibare's hybrid textile installations propose a new cultural exchange staged within a postcolonial space. These installations offer a variety of meanings and readings: colonisation and trade, the hand-made and the ready-made, origin and authenticity, self and other, and gender and ethnicity are richly investigated. These readings and orchestration of differing elements collide and excite at the very edges of postcolonial discourse within a complex translation of conventional artistic hierarchies and orthodoxies.

What is at stake here? What are the implications of these 'innovative' hybrid textile forms that draw, with apparent ease and confidence, on notions of the domestic and the decorative, gender and the rhetorics of a (modernist) art history?

Born in London in 1962, Yinka Shonibare grew up in postcolonial Nigeria with his parents, returning to Britain to finish off A levels and to go to art college. In our recent interview, he says: 'I have always been in this position of shuttling between two geographies, two cultures and speaking two languages: Yoruba at home and English at school since this was the official language of institutions... The legacy of colonialism throughout the current education system was very present because English is the official language. And so you grow up kind of looking up to Britain even if it's an ambivalent relationship.'[3]

This ambivalent relationship to Britain was foregrounded during his years studying art at Goldsmiths College. As he puts it, 'as somebody who actually grew up in a city (Lagos) it was quite strange that I was expected to have some knowledge of Nigerian culture in a way which has actually been lost or diluted. As an African student in inverted commas, I was under pressure to produce, in inverted commas, something ethnic.'

In 1990 Yinka Shonibare started to work with 'African' fabric which he bought in the markets in Brixton, an inner-city area of south-west London. These fabrics have a complicated set of histories that precisely unravel definitions of origin and authenticity and run parallel to Shonibare's own questioning of selfhood. Without mapping the travel routes of these 'African' fabrics there is no point of entry into Shonibare's work and the questions it raises about postcolonial experience and the cultural effects of transculturalism.

Given the transcultural history of batik, Shonibare comments on the irony of asserting African, or Nigerian, culture by wearing batik prints: 'the irony of the whole thing is that, post-independence, Nigerians who wanted to assert themselves, assert Nigerian culture against British culture, would actually wear traditional dress and in many cases that would be in the batik. Because living now in London and chiefly in Brixton, if people wanted to express some kind of sense of African nationalism, they would wear batik. They might wear head wraps and then wear just Western clothes.'

Batik, commonly known in Western Europe as 'African' fabric, is a Javanese term of wax-resist dyeing. Coming from Indonesia, hand-block imitation batiks and fancy prints (the term used for factory-produced textiles printed on one side of the cloth) were manufactured in Europe from the mid-nineteenth century as part of the swelling European textile industry. As early as 1846, the batik prints produced by the Netherlands company Vlisco (Van Vissinger Helmond) were essential to the development of Dutch colonialism. In the United kingdom, the Manchester company ABC (Arthur Brunnschweiler and Company) was rival to Vlisco in the textile trade.[4] Strictly speaking, not all the batiks or wax-resist prints produced in

Manchester and subsequently in Africa are batiks at all, as some are prints which reproduce the batik imagery, and so can be read as surrogates or stand-ins for an inauthentic textile and national identity.

ABC also produced so-called 'Java prints' for export to colonial West Africa. Along with chintz fabric, these prints had a commercial viability as they became increasingly popular for traditional dress which both served and subverted the pretensions of Empire. It is ironic that prints which were initially set for engraving in 1909 could come to signify precolonial 'traditional' culture. Subsequently, local industries, particularly in Ghana, were established to produce indigenous fabrics. On the one hand, batiks produced outside of this production environment operated as a sign of high status and investment value. On the other hand, production inside West Africa was viewed as a competitive alternative to colonial imports using exported European cottons to manufacture 'African resists'. As Shonibare wryly explains:

> There began a sort of commissioning system between Africa and Manchester. If there was an important occasion, like the visiting of a president, they could actually have their portraits incorporated into the design of the fabrics and these fabrics would be printed in Manchester and distributed to Africa. [5]

What is significant here is that the batik fabrics serve as mobile signs which refuse a final signified or final destination. In Europe they evoke an exotic/erotic 'African' otherness; in Africa they operate as a sign of aspiration through the allure of imported goods; and in postindependent Nigeria they are a popular expression of postcolonial nationalism. As adopted by young British blacks, these textiles become symbols of Afro pride and identity.

Observing that 'the material which is being used to assert this sense of nationalism itself is very hybrid', Shonibare's use of batik articulates the *complexity and plurality* of black British identity. As Kobena Mercer has commented, a defining characteristic of black Britain is 'the broad-based shift away from essentialist views of blackness as a unitary identity fixed in the authenticity of one's origins, towards a more relational view of the plural identities constructed from the Caribbean, South Asia and African migrations of the post-war era'. [6]

Because Empire brought together disparate peoples, whether as colonial subjects or as coloured immigrants, blackness in Britain has always been a more heterogeneous, composite and hybrid affair than it is in the United States.

While the 1980s advocacy for Afro-Asian alliances under a shared signifier of blackness no longer has currency, Mercer argues that 'a pluralist approach to the cultural politics of taci and ethnicity nonetheless remains peculiar to black British perspectives in the arts'. Adopting a pluralistic outlook, black British artists began to use the polyvocal character of their experience in order to speak as a minority representative.

In this context the modernist notion of kitsch, against which Clement Greenberg was indignant, is subject to critical and aesthetic revision. Indeed, Donald John Cosentino coins the term 'Afrokitsch' to describe the use of kitsch in the art of everyday life, arguing that an 'enthusiasm for simulacra' is directly attributable to the demand for kitsch after Nigerian independence in 1960.[7] Greenberg's argument against kitsch was a moral one; he saw kitsch as a 'gigantic apparition, content-driven and appealing to the masses who have always been indifferent to culture'. Seemingly full of devices, tricks and strategies, kitsch derives its life-blood from a reserving of accumulated experience. For Greenberg, kitsch was the epitome of that which is spurious in the life of our time. But it could be argued that the adoption of 'African' batiks might be evidence of an 'uplifting' kitsch, to use Cosentino's term, since the 'traditional' symbol of 'African' fabric is co-opted to promote a political and national agenda. It is this possibility that Susan Sontag opens up with her observation that kitsch has a strategic advantage in lending itself to variety and mimicry, thereby subverting conventions of 'good taste' and moral superiority.[5]

The hybridity of batik and the adoption of Afrokitsch combine with the 'enthusiasm for simulacra', evident particularly in areas like Brixton, to stimulate an urban imaginary. Yinka Shonibare's work is part of the transcultural project which undermines the essentialism of the Greenbergian position. This greater sense of the complexity and hybridity is critical to a postcolonial perspective which, as Stuart Hall suggests, has directed our attention to the many ways in which colonialisation was never simply external to the societies of the imperial metropolis but rather it was always deeply inscribed within them, at one and the same time as it became deeply and indelibly inscribed on the colonised. As a consequence, Hall argues, there is no return to a pure set of uncontaminated origins since the long-term historical and cultural effects of 'transculturalism' are irreversible.

Questions of hybridity and cultural undecidability (questions foreshadowed in Jacques Derrida's writing) are forefronted in thinking through the complexities of diasporic experience to the extent that any 'return' to ethnically closed or centred 'original' histories is untenable and marked by movements across global/local inter-relationships. The interweaving of these relationships is played out through a critical interruption in which the 'story of capital and trade is centred from a European perspective as opposed to new ways of conceptualising the ebb and flow of cultural exchange'.[9] It is this ebb and flow of cultural exchange in the history of postcolonial Africa and Britain, and the complexities of black British culture, that infuse Yinka Shonibare's work. Informed by his interest in the writing of Roland Barthes and Jacques Derrida, Shonibare also pinpoints the point at which the personal becomes political:

> But what I then started to do was to understand that my own personal history, which makes me bilingual, is somehow linked to the kind of colonial experience... and so I decided to work on what I knew.

In 1995 Shonibare staged three mannequins dressed in bustled Victorian crinolines. They were exquisitely tailored by Sian Lewis; the brightly coloured batiks were industrially produced by ABC in Manchester. These three mannequins were shown together as 'How does a girl like you, get to be a girl like you?' in *The Art of African Textiles: Technology, Tradition and Lurex* held at the Barbican Art Gallery, London, in November/December 1995, *Sensation* at the Royal Academy in London six months later, and most notably in *Jurassic Technologies* in Sydney, Australia in summer 1996. A later work, 'Dressing Down' (1997), also uses these boldly patterned, industrially produced fancy prints. The frilly crinolines produce highly decorative effects, signifying both the former ruling-class power and the status accorded to detailed (and female with all its associations of the feminine) 'tailored' labour.

Shonibare's strategy of decorating and embellishing his 'dresses' produces aesthetic pleasure that parodies a Victorian life-style as just that – mere style. This acceptance of aesthetic pleasure, in making the works as well as viewing them, is part of Shonibare's strategy. He comments that 'I think I would describe myself as an aesthete because I like colour and I like really beautiful things but I also like the paradox of being known as a conceptual artist who is of essentially visual. The visual is provocative and at the same it actually questions things I get passionate about':

> I'm actually using pleasure and seduction as a subversive mode, in the way that you can actually use it as a provocative guise. Josephine Baker comes to mind in the way she uses this kind of provocative dance to empower herself through a stereotype of the ethnic dancer. She did this provocative banana dance which was very popular but she also made a lot of money doing it as she so empowered herself through the use of cultural stereotyping.

Shonibare uses ornamentation to effect this combination of pleasure and provocation. In his discussion on ornament, Mick Carter observes that ornament, with all its associations of adornment and decoration, has a tendency to wander and not stay in its 'proper place' and that this errancy can threaten the aesthetic value of an entire work.[10] (Carter's treatment of ornament recalls Kant's discussion of ornament in *Critique of Judgement*.) Shonibare uses this errancy to telling effect since he re-stages the whole order of the ornamental and the decorative, by re-working the scene as a fantastical encounter between the exotic 'other' of the colonially displaced merged with the frippery of a nineteenth-century Victorian crinoline, in a hybridic fantasy of artificial seduction.

Shonibare's crinolines remind viewers that clothing has always functioned historically as a regulatory mechanism which not only shapes the body but ensures confirmation of social and psychic norm. But, as Kaja Silverman argues, the network of symbolic relations which are signified by clothing are never finally fixed. In Silverman's analysis, clothing not only articulates the body to make a subject but it is also vulnerable to subversion and re-signification. Shonibare achieves this re-signification with his parody of Victorian dresses. He comments that he found crinolines sexy and they fulfilled part of his desire to titillate the viewer.

It seems highly appropriate that Victorian dresses are used for vehicles of seduction in this way since, in part, these 'textile' installations are indebted to feminist strategies and to Rosemarie Trockel's influence, which Shonibare acknowledges. In Trockel's 'textile' garments of knitted readymades, ontological gender codes are destabilised. Trockel plays jokes as does Shonibare since 'we' are lured into a semantic field of ambiguous sexual desire. Are we being dressed down in subversive laughter? Who, plays the tricks on whom? There is, I think, an erotic femininity at play here, but it is not directed towards any specific object but rather directed towards a fantasy signalling gender trouble and identity dislocation. I am reminded of an 1853 *Punch* cartoon depicting a Victorian maid dressed in a crinoline. Servants dressing up in the manner of their mistresses was a recurring theme found in many cartoons in Britain in the nineteenth century.[11] If servants imitate their 'elders' and 'betters', wearing elaborate frocks and aspiring to frilly ornaments beyond 'their' station, then the signs of aristocracy are undone.

These Victorian dresses, and particularly the excessive bustle, represent the old vestiges of Empire as no more than their own exotic bric-à-brac. At the same time they provide for the possibility of new fantasies in which even the 'identity' of the wearer can mimic the forms and rhythm of the 'old' as a radical cut-and-mix of social and sexual hierarchies.

Both 'How does a girl like you, get to be a girl like you?' and 'Dressing Down' are rich in irony and mischief. The organic, ornamental flurries of 'African' batiks blended with bustled Victorian crinolines stand in for aristocratic trappings in a scene of comic exaggeration. A scene full of cultural impunity may signify sexual impurity. The shape of the crinolines in 'Dressing Down' denotes the decorum expected of Victorian ladies but the 'batiks', with their hot colours and gaudy patterns, masquerade their wares in a 'blur of the received demarcating lines between them'. Sarat Maharaj asks, 'does the Eurocentric gaze gain a further lease of life in this masquerade, in the guise of the 'Ethnic' look? Does the letter simply mime and endorse the former, a straightforward mirroring and celebration of Eurocentric textile-fashion-costume construction of otherness?'[12] Shonibare plays off notions of the original and copied item with generous naughtiness. He enjoys the fact that 'the dresses, with the bustles and everything, are sexy and provocative because of the big bottoms and so on'. At the very moment when viewers are being drawn to seductive, aesthetic pleasure, Shonibare beguiles them into considering political issues. However, a crucial in-between space is created for selfinvention and self-reflectivity and it is one in which the dynamics of cultural difference lie in dialogic exchange.

When 'How does a girl like you, get to be a girl like you?' and 'Dressing Down' are juxtaposed with 'Feather Pink' and 'Deep Blue' (both 1996/7) a further set of issues emerge. These issues refer to the ways in which 'pure' abstraction has been polluted by extra-pictorial qualities of all things associated with the decorative and applied arts. Positioned as the 'other' to Clement Greenberg's patrolling and policing of borders and boundaries of self-enclosed disciplines, decoration, in the guise of amoebic 'textile' patterns, returns to haunt modern painting. Yinka Shonibare's delight in playing off references to Greenberg's famous diction in 1961 was that 'the essence of modernism lies... in the use of the characteristic methods of the discipline not in order to subvert it, but to entrench it more firmly in its area of competence'[13]

For Greenberg, self-referential autonomy, which was to be achieved by a scrupulous attention to the specifics of that practice, assumed that it was possible to draw boundaries around the aesthetic 'frame'. Greenberg's view was based on a moral judgement: 'purity in art' was a means of preserving a living, Western culture. Preservation and purity were qualities marshalled to defend extra-pictorial pollution. Shonibare acknowledges that he is 'definitely challenging Greenberg's modernist notions of purity, polluting that pure space with crafts'. He sees his use of batik as drawing 'low culture in inverted commas' and 'tacky crafts' into the 'so-called high art space'.

Whether it is Gary Hume's love of the details of tapestry flora and fauna or Chris Ofili's lashings of scrumptious paint, many contemporary British artists flirt with decorative possibilities in practices for which it was once taboo. Detail, the minute and intricate attention to pattern and paternity are acknowledged as having the potential to subvert an internal, hierarchic ordering of surface structure. The detail – and note that in Yinka Shonibare's work, the detail explodes across the cloth – also participates in a larger semantic field bonded on one side by the ornamental, with its connotation of effeminacy and decadence, and on the other by the everyday, whose 'prosiness' is rooted in the domestic sphere of social life presided over by women.[14] In his painting, too, Shonibare contests the gendered groundrules of modernist art by breaking down the 'large heroic male, large male heroic canvas into kind of fragments so there's actually a kind of literal breaking down that's kind of happening there'.

'We all engage with a notion of what's margin, what's centre,' he says. Shonibare's considered engagement with semiotics pays off well. After all, knowing the code and signs, when playing off-side and mimicking back, Shonibare takes the idea of clothing to question assumptions about the ethnicity of these garments. It is like the mirror was turned back. We can no longer say 'who I am'; rather we ask 'who are you?' Similarly, in his painting, he resists 'staying in some kind of closed ethnic territory' to 'cross over to a kind of postmodern territory'. Like the Victorian dresses, the texture of the paint and the model's expression become a code:

> Obviously people can see that the Victorian dress is not African. But then I cross the so-called boundary that is actually set out for me into this territory. But in a way what I then do is ethnicise the aristocracy.

Whilst 'How does a girl like you, get to be a girl like you?' and 'Dressing Down' are key works in Shonibare's personal inter-cultural history, and aesthetic, material practice, it is arguably 'A Victorian Philanthropist's Parlour' which opens up the greatest possibility of dislocating and exposing the viewer to further questions around cultural identity through tracing the origins of African batik fabrics.

In December 1996, Shonibare's 'A Victorian Philanthropist's Parlour', especially commissioned by London Printworks Trust, opened to the public for the first time as part of LPT's exhibition programme, *Pledge Allegiance to a Flag?*. For this exhibition Shonibare researched Victorian interiors with the help of the Victoria and Albert and the Geffrye museums. As Shonibare himself acknowledges, LPT provided him with a unique opportunity to shift the scale and complexity of his work through a combination of intrictate public funding and technical expertise. LPT is a unique educational and cultural organisation dedicated to commission new work from artists and designers through collaborative residencies at the project's textile printing open-access facilties in Brixton. Artists selected are chosen to reflect the diversity of applications associated with the medium of printed textiles and to reflect the cultural diversity of the project's home in South London. This is a multi-culturally diverse area of south east London where 'ethnic minorities' make up 20% of the population in a fusion of fast food, world music and traditional markets; the same markets where Shonibare often buys his fabrics. The exhibition's brief for *Pledge Allegiance to a Flag?*, to which Yinka Shonibare was invited to respond, called for an investigation:

> ...a national flag is a complex symbol; the anachronistic notion of an administrative flag as marker of borders and a symbol of national unity and national celebration is still perpetuated. A contemporary view sees a national flag as a complex symbol: repatriation, sports, politics, world demographic change and patterns of human development, are all issues likely to affect a 1996 reading of these highly charged pieces of fabric.

Shonibare, exploring his own natural kind of instinct against the flag, with its legacies of nationalism and colonialism, explained: 'I don't want to produce a literal flag but I want to look at notions of allegiances and sport. Football seems to be a place where you know people feel really high passions about their allegiances. You know I mean not only in sports because it also becomes a way of getting out, another sign of upward social mobility. I wanted to kind of look at these issues as I had with the dresses before'.

Shonibare's research led him to to the Geffrye Museum in the East End of London. It is a museum which I frequent often as it was once an eighteenth-century building and alms houses of the Ironmongers' Company, located in the heart of London's East End where I live. The Geffrye Museum opened in 1914 as a furniture museum and until the 1980s showed room interiors of the British middle classes from 1600 to 1939. Currently the museum consists of a number of rooms for different periods: an Elizabethan room, a Stuart room, a William and Mary room, an early Georgian, a late Georgian and a Regency room, a mid-Victorian room, the Voysey room (c.1910), a 1930s room and a 1950s suburban lounge. Since the late 1980s and early 1990s, the museum has focused on the previously neglected histories of women, working-class life, and the effect of Empire on London's economy. These intimate but complex histories explore the impact of Africa, Asia and the Caribbean on British life and the contributions made by black people in Britain during colonialisation. The project with Yinka Shonibare – to develop the Victorian Philanthropist's Parlour – was one of the first between the museum, LPT as a the commissioning body, and an artist, to specifically address these issues.

As an outsider one looks in on a room full of rich furnishings, curved and heavily upholstered furniture, where ornaments decorate every shelf and flat surface available in a tightly controlled space stuffed to the brim with cushions, carpets, curtains and rugs. This room in the Geffrye Museum is labelled mid-Victorian, around 1870. It is known as a front parlour. Important guests were received in a room like this, one in which the furnishings expressed the taste and wealth of the family; a middle-class family or rather the new middle-class whose Victorian things travelled the roads and seas of the Empire. As Shonibare recalled and as I know, a middle-class family viewed their nineteenth-century home as a repository of feeling, sincerity, honesty, truth and love seemingly lost or denied in the world outside, or so Adrian Forty argues.[15] The home provided a sanctuary, and acted as a base of moral welfare, from all things that might corrupt such a family of virtue. Forty goes further to suggest that the home was turned into a place of unreality; a template for the new aspiring middle class to borrow models of aristocratic life with its connotations of freedom from work, design and love of beauty. This place, a mid-Victorian home turned into a place of unreality, a place where illusions flourish, did not escape Sonibare's mischievous eye as part of his project not only to ethnicise the aristocracy but also to explore the aspirations of the middle class to mimic them.

On entering the Victorian parlour, as it is arranged in the museum, you can observe two details that Shonibare borrowed for his contemporary re-interpretation. One is the mass-produced wallpaper, designed by Owen Jones, superintendent of the Great Exhibition of 1851 and author of *The Grammar of Ornament* (1856); the other is the exterior of Crystal Palace, the temporary 'home' of the Great Exhibition, embroidered on the firescreen and placed at the centre of the parlour's hearth.

On viewing Shonibare's version of 'A Victorian Philanthropist's Parlour' (colour plate no. 13) it is the ornamental wallpaper that holds attention. Yet again surfaces were playfully decorated with textile designs popular in West Africa. The colour strikes one most, with changing 'moods' of mid-Victorian crimsons and golds, hot oranges and blues with green/yellow in full-bodied shades flowing across every conceivable surface of an opulent interior from the wallpaper to the fabricated furniture and a mocked-up imitation of an

Yinka Shonibare
A Victorian Philanthropist's Parlour (1997)
installation: printed fabrics: London Printworks, Brixton, London

Axminster pile-carpet. Within the twirls and flurries of the printed cloth, there are images of black football players 'in action' playing for Europe. The addition of footballers, all of whom are of African and Caribbean descent, running in and out of the batik designs in European shirts and badges, further disrupt the comforts of the parlour. Walk around the edge and it is evidently a stage set. The DIY carpentry literally props up a duplicated Victorian interior, haunting and flaunting an excessive theatricality in a confident, peacock display of flirtatious seduction. A photograph of Crystal Palace and the Great Exhibition of 1851 is lodged on the mantelshelf as part of the clutter of collectibles. These provide bookends to the bust of Queen

Victoria that stands at the shelf's centre. These curios are orchestrated within a spectacle of fantasy and erotic charge invested in the mottled background of an inviting *chaise longue*. Nonetheless, it is the re-importation and strategic use of 'ethnic' fabric, jazzy 'African' batiks, oozing confidence in transparent splendour, that strikes 'home', just as the signature stitched into the firescreen is that of one of the first black British footballers to play for England, John Barnes, replacing the temporary 'home' of the Great Exhibition embroidered on the 'orginal' firescreen and placed at the centre of the parlour's hearth.

For Shonibare, fabric and significantly newly created African batiks, encompass a hybridic practice which takes recognisable textile motifs and processes and empties them out. He fills them with new content to create a complicated allegory, an experience of experience which is culturally mixed through a mosaic of different languages and aesthetic strategies. Often autobiographical, Shonibare (in my view) positions himself somewhere in a shuttling process of constant translation. The dynamics of cultural difference lie not in the analogies of tradition, Homi Bhabha has argued, nor in the retrieval of tradition as some kind of archival commodity, but in the metaphoric models of enunciation and negotiation.

By playing, mimicking, ridiculing and flirting with the origins and metaphors of African textiles, Shonibare continually probes and negotiates his own identity, exposing it as unfixed, as hybrid. By dressing down textiles in 'A Victorian Philanthropist's Parlour', Shonibare engages us with the dynamics of cultural difference; the overlap and tensions between the textile metaphors and signs, serve to create a future with no fixed, final signified. Ideas of tradition and innovation are challenged in material practice through an unfixing of the fixed category of art at the same time as the idea of fixed identity is destabilised via a strategy of what he calls 'purloined seduction or pretend authenticity'. We are all undone and dressed down.

Notes

1. Yinka Shonibare quoted in Kobena Mercer, 'Art That Is Ethnic In Inverted Commas: on Yinka Shonibare', *Frieze* 35, Nov./Dec. 1995, pp. 38–41.
2. Oguibe Olu, 'A Brief Note on Internationalism', in *Global Visions: Towards a New Internationalism in the Visual Arts* (ed. Jean Fisher), Kala Press, London, 1994, pp. 50–59.
3. Yinka Shonibare, interview with the author, London, Feb. 1998. Other quotes are also from this interview, unless given a specific reference.
4. See section on factory-printed textiles in *The Art of African Textiles: Technology, Tradition and Lurex* (ed. John Picton), ex. cat., Lund Humphries and Barbican Art Gallery, London, 1995, p. 24.
5. Yinka Shonibare, 'Fabric, and the Irony of Authenticity', *Annotations 1, Mixed Belongings*

and Unspecified Destinations (ed. Nikos Papastergiadis), Institute of International Visual Arts, London, p. 41.

6.   Kobena Mercer, 'Back to my routes: A postscript to the 80s', ex. cat., *Pictura Britannica Art from Britain*, Museum of Contemporary Art, Sydney, 1997, pp. 119–120.

7.   Donald John Cosentino, 'Afrokitsch', *Africa Explores: 20th Century African Art*, Centre for African Art, New York and Prestel (ed. Susan Vogel), Munich, 1993, pp. 240–256.

8.   Susan Sontag, 'Notes on Camp', in *A Susan Sontag Reader*, introduction by Elizabeth Hardwick (Penguin reprint, London) 1992, pp. 105–121.

9.   Stuart Hall, 'When was the Post-colonial: Thinking at the Limit' in *The Post-Colonial Reader* (eds Ian Chambers and Linda Curti), Routledge, London, 1996, pp. 242–262.

10.   Mick Carter, *Putting a Face on Things: Studies in Imaginary Materials*, Power Institute, Sydney, 1997, particularly the chapter 'Ornament and the Ornamental' (pp. 117 –152). See also: Kaja Silverman, 'Fragments of a Fashionable Discourse', *Studies in Entertainment: Critical approaches to Mass Culture* (ed. Tania Modelski), University of Indiana Press, Bloomington. 1986, p. 147.

11.   *Punch, vol. 24, 1853*; reproduced in Adrian Forty, *Objects of Desire: Design and Society 1750–1980*, Thames and Hudson, London, 1987, p. 170.

12.   Sarat Maharaj, 'Arachne's Genre: Towards Inter-Cultural Studies in Textiles', *Journal of Design History*, vol.4, no. 2, 1991, p. 91.

13.   Francis Frascina, *Pollock and After: The Critical Debate*, Harper & Row, London, 1985.

14.   See Naomi Schor, *Reading in Detail: Aesthetics and the Feminine*, Methuen, London,1987.

15.   Adrian Forty, *Objects of Desire: Design and Society 1750–1980*, pp. 101–102. See also Asa Briggs, *Victorian Things*, Penguin, London, 1988.

TEXTILES AS VIEWFINDER:
SUSIE BRANDT + QUOTIDIAN + CLOTH

Margo Mensing

Neither preciousness nor durability of material are prerequisites...
Any material, any working procedure,
and any method of production, manual or industrial,
can serve an end that may be art.
Anni Albers, *On Weaving*

Susie Brandt's woven wall hanging, 'After Albers' (1998), reiterates a double-weave wall hanging (1927) by Anni Albers [see colour plate no. 6]. Within the grid divided into rows of squares, Albers individualised each square, making it unique through its alignment of horizontal and vertical lines. In the black-and-white photograph in *On Weaving*, this weaving reproduces achromatically in multiple greys, blacks and whites. Brandt worked directly from this photograph in creating her version which repeats the lines and tones in the original Albers weaving. In 'After Albers' Brandt used discarded pantyhose rather than yarn. She also deviated from the original in not using the loom but a small metal frame, an item which is usually packaged with nylon loops and sold as a kit for children to weave potholders.

Brandt's copy can scarcely be called a copy; it is an original pantyhose potholder wall hanging imitating the design of Anni Albers. Brandt's weaving sounds dreadful; it looks good. Neither pantyhose nor potholder is immediately identifiable. Only close inspection reveals individual potholders which correspond to each of Albers' squares. Even closer inspection is necessary to realise that Brandt has replaced the kit's nylon loops with pantyhose. Susie Brandt makes her version look like the original but the substituted material and construction method rephrase Albers's Bauhaus aesthetic. While Albers espoused openness to materials, Brandt's choice of panthose would likely have been strange in the mind of the modernist. Strange, but not unconscionable.

I begin with this example of Susie Brandt's work because it refers to the legacy of Anni Albers, exemplar of modernism and mother of us all. Here I refer to American textile artists trained in art history and theory and in the construction and history of textiles. Brandt, in her quilts and blankets, takes common objects and reworks them. The resulting polished retrofits retain their identity as quilts or blankets but subvert the meaning of their classification. Brandt is grounded in textiles; an orientation she shares with Albers. By this I mean, textiles are her viewfinder, a lens she focuses to sharpen her surroundings. The first field that comes into sight is that of the textile itself. In this looped, reductivist view, Brandt uses textiles to look at textiles. Brandt joins one element to the next seamlessly – that overused adverb lifted from the seamstress's world. She constructs fields of information by seamlessly connecting congruent but unexpected elements into unlikely fabrics.

Looking at a sampling of Brandt's textile works reveals that the quotidian, the commonplace, is the source for her quilts and blankets. However, Brandt's work is not all textile work; she also produces installations. The quotidian is as pervasive in the installations as it is in the textile works. In her ordering and compiling of the installations, Brandt expands her use of textiles. Here too textiles provide the viewfinder. Borrowing and recasting found materials, Brandt assembles her quotidian finds using textile methods of construction and metaphors. The works themselves question attitudes on land use as well as craft traditions. She resituates the paraphernalia of daily life and in so doing offers an alternative to the canonical position of American craft which developed in the 1970s. She is not, of course, alone in this endeavour. Delight in the found object is a prominent strain in twentieth-century art making. Understood from the viewpoint of a textile artist, she becomes a case study of the craftsman as provocateur.

Quotidian and vernacular mean essentially the same thing – the commonplace – but they most often appear in different contexts. Quotidian is coupled with the objects of daily life. Vernacular, originally attached to language and meaning the vulgar or common language, is frequently used in connection with architecture and extends to encompass the landscape. Brandt works in this territory humorously, picking through the detritus of daily life for its ironies. There is nothing worshipful in her scavenging. A different course sees the everyday infused with the spiritual. Historically American craft has travelled this path creating a myth that views the land as sacred, a premise explicated in Mary Douglas's *The Craftsman as Yeoman: Myth and Cultural Identity in American Craft*.[1]Because much of Brandt's work originates in contrary views on land use, Brandt's installations use textiles as a viewfinder to point out the imprint of the vernacular. The lens keeps telescoping: textiles provide the focus, but the view widens to encompass historical attitudes about the land and the role of the craftsperson. I will discuss each of these three topics derived from the social role of textiles.

Textiles and the Quotidian

Anni Albers (1899–1994) is a good place to begin and to end because of her lifelong commitment to textiles. She believed in the homogeneity of art, craft and design. She enjoyed a long life, one that almost spanned the twenthieth century. Emigrating from Germany in 1933, Josef and Anni Albers taught at Black Mountain College from 1933 to 1949. The Albers disseminated the theory and practice of the Bauhaus in America. Anni Albers is identified with textiles, and more particularly, weaving. Though she abandoned the loom in favour, of printmaking in the 1960s, Anni Albers made her mark on art, craft and design through her loom production and her writings. Her career comcides with High Modernism with its emphasis on progress and perfection, the design and manufacture.of streamlined goods to benefit humankind. Anni Albers operated continually in both art and design. During her years at the Bauhaus in Dessau, Germany, Albers designed and hand-wove samples for industrial production. She knew well how to construct a functional textile made of quality materials. Immersed in the rapid changes of the developing machine technology, Albers of designed textiles destined to improve everyday life.

When Albers turned to the everyday, she claimed 'any material, any working procedure, and any method of production' as the province of art. Her inclusiveness was not so much a comment on consumerism as a willingness to transform any material or object and elevate it to the status of art. It can 'serve an end that may be art'. She sometimes used found materials gathered from nature. At other times she incorporated manufactured items. The ready-made with its premise that anything can serve as art might occasionally appear in her work. Yet discards, the cheap, and the rejected were used for their design properties rather than for social commentary. Mary Jane Jacobs points outl that Albers's 'unprejudiced use of materials' led her to innovative solutions serving 'both functional and esthetic'.[2]

From her earliest Banhaus studies Anni Albers delighted in the inherent properties of textiles, appreciated their tactile qualities, and respected their specific laws of production.

Brandt's work is likewise informed by textiles. She is typical of many artists who seize the disdained and discarded. Price and convenience are two reasons for her choice of materials. Pantyhose, silk flowers, cheap new manufactured lace – all record the glut of the market and the contents of the back of the dresser drawer. Brandt's individual fabric pieces, such as

'After Albers' [see colour plate no. 6b], 'Dainty', or the 'Peek-a-boo' quilts, ironically reconfigure the stuff of which they are made. Material laboriously transformed and category equated with function are central to Susie Brandt's perspective. She transforms material without disguising it. Upon close inspection, or better, through handling, the viewer discerns properties of the specific elements which combine into the whole. On the other hand, category recognition – this is a quilt or a blanket – is apparent from first glance. Brandt has thoroughly worked out the slippage between these two operatives. She constructs her own textiles which are reconstructed originals. The past and the present are inextricably mated in each work. Whatever arena she works in, Brandt questions the appropriate through insertion of the inappropriate.

The quotidian in art is often the wholesale incorporation of everyday things into accumulations that comment on consumer culture, practised, for example, by Arman. Arman's early installations, such as 'Le Plein' (Full Up) in 1960, suggest the influence of Marxist philosopher Henri Lefebvre who believed capitalism of his day no longer centred on production but consumption. Seizing the everyday, Arman's installations depended upon chaos. Susie Brandt's materials are leftovers and discards, but the form is orderly. This fits Albers and the textile format more than Arman's grazing, but Brandt is reflecting upon a consumerist economy as well as mirroring it in choosing quilting with its origins and reasons for being in recycle and reuse. Brandt is only marginally interested in the sanctity of thrift. Quantity is more intriguing than quality and her view of value is all-inclusive. She is interested in what is available, and what is available is usually what most people don't want. One of craft's central tenets has been the preservation and use of natural materials. In a fine reversal, Brandt gathers from all of society's manufacture.

In 'Dainty' (1991–2) she started with old lace, sewing over and over the holes until diaphanous can no longer be associated with lace. Repeated stitching obliterates existing lace, creating a new lace. Heavy folds reference drapery not lace curtains. This transmogrified fabric asks whether lace is meant to cover or uncover. An engaging textile, Brandt believes, must visually challenge the viewer by changing as s/he draws closer to it. The nature of lace construction with its open and closed units offers multiple sites for these changes to take place. Lace can be manipulated to accentuate covering or uncovering. The fabric's symbolic significance is another reason for its appeal. The bridal veil, a Madeira tablecloth and napkins represent what we most appreciate in textiles – purity, elegance, cleanliness.

Lace is not, however, a fabric or a construction mode that is associated with quilting. Intended for the bed, quilts are meant to be sturdy and serviceable. Brandt sews machine-made lace in her quilt series, 'Peek-a-boo'. Abundantly available, machine lace is cheap. Like most commodities, the price of lace has everything to do with time. Hand lace-making tops the list of labour-intensive textile production. Expensive fibres such as silk and flax also affect the price. In machine lace, synthetics keep the price low. Brandt demonstrates in 'Peek-a-boo' that the devalued can be valuable when carefully and cleverly refashioned. Thought and action bring us back to the worth of the hand.

First shown at St Peter's Church in New York, the 'Peek-a-Boo' lace quilts register from a distance as traditional quilt patterns – Drunkard's Path, Flying Geese, Sunshine and Shadow. Only by focusing the lens on material does Frederick's of Hollywood reveal itself; one realises that warmth is not the point. This lace suggests more readily what is worn to bed than bed cover. Dismissed is any pretence of covering up, and, therefore, comfort – the prime function of the quilt. Also dismissed is nostalgia. Romancing the past is not Brandt's intention. When revisiting the past she inserts the vernacular to imprint the present. The possibility (or limit) of nostalgia is inherent in the quilt, but her recontextualisation of form through material stifles it. Her choice of everyday, unappealing, used or cheap goods all works to deflate the spatce of everyday life as sacred or spiritual. Although the effectiveness of Brandt's reconfigured textiles depends on using vast quantities of one kind of thing, what matters most is not the choice of a particular but the onslaught of material.

'Adirondackland': Installation and the Quotidian

This same resourceful gathering and compiling is present in Brandt's installations. She appropriates vernacular source material from a particular locality in order to comment on land use. Knowledge of the history of a place is essential if social commentary is to have any effect. Brandt's choice of particular place is Adirondack Park, New York.[3] Her personal history is embedded in the history of the Park and this has formed her ironic view of the tangled ideals and realities of land use. The diverse population living in the Park is further complicated by the seasonal influx of tourists. 'The wilderness' turns out to be not nature's preserve but a layered mixed-use site.

Adirondack Park is over six million acres. A state-owned preserve, it is almost as large as the State of Massachusetts. The ideal of the national park system, and by extension that of the individual states, is to reverse private property holdings, converting the land within the boundaries back to the public domain. The reality of Adirondack Park is that more than half the

Susie Brandt
Adirondackland (1995)
NYS Biennial, NYS Museum, Albany, NY
mixed-media installation, fire ring and tent

Park's area is in private hands and will probably remain there. Its mountainous and forested terrain make it a favourite hiking and camping spot but, it is not all or even half wilderness. There are numerous towns and much industry within its boundaries. In Corinth, Brandt's town, the nearby prison and the paper mill are the chief employers.

The human history of the Park is a key to Brandt's dichotomous attitude towards craft which reverberates between outright irreverence and respectful attention. It is clearly seen in Susie Brandt's response to the three economies of the Adirondacks – logging, tourism, and manufacturing, especially paper pulp and textiles. *Adirondackland* (1995) [see colour plate no. 7] is a collaborative venture of Susie and her sister, Betsy. Opening at Art-in-General, a non-profit gallery in New York City, the installation moved to two other New York State locations – the New York State Museum, Albany (the state capital), and St Lawrence University, Canton, far north in Adirondack Park, near the Canadian border.

The gallery space in *Adirondackland* contained two sites. The first was a souvenir shop, where Brandt-manufactured souvenirs could be purchased. The second was a simulated clearing in the woods. Both installation sites, the souvenir shop and the clearing in the woods, reconstructed the museum device of historical room or tableau. Two life-styles were pivotal: recreation, and logging. In each setting, the tree stump served as icon.

The souvenir shop was housed in a typical Adirondack-style white tent. The merchandise included: postcards picturing tree stumps from several perspectives; tree stump cuddle toys made of camouflage-print velour; simulated gilt cardboard clocks imitating a slice of crosscut log; small mesh bags of potpourri (designated with the brand name *Adirondackscents*) filled with bottle caps, balsam needles, leaves, and cigarette butts. The souvenir shop at the Art-in-General location functioned most faithfully to meld merchandise and art because visitors actually did have to pass through the shop to enter or exit the installation. At this New York City venue the elevator opened directly into the store and the guard doubled as sales clerk. That a museum's identity is as bound up in its retail space as its gallery space is a given; for example, many go to the Museum of Modern Art only to shop. There are no admission tickets needed to enter the store. The *Adirondackland* gift store-souvenir mimicked the architectural footprint of museums today.

By creating a store, the Brandts became entrepreneurs, they entered the art marketplace within the not-for-profit sector. They deployed considerable merchandising skill in reinventing stock items packaged for Adirondack tourist spots. They borrowed ideas for their souvenir items from the store attached to Adirondack Museum in Blue Mountain. More unlikely are the items they appropriated from the drive-by opportunity of Park residents' front yards. Their choice of the unsavoury – cigarette butts to replicate birch twigs – conflated the disdained with the emulated in a surprisingly appealing product. Lucy Lippard observes that:

the notion of the local, the locale, the location, the locality, the place in art, however, has not caught on in the mainstream because in order to attract sufficient buyers in the current system of distribution, art must be relatively generalized, detachable from politics and pain.[4]

This was not true in *Adirondackland* where shoppers purchased and the Brandts pocketed profit. They demonstrated that cheap goods, attractively constructed and well packaged, sold in quantity, can provide income for artists. This runs counter to standards for high craft.

The Brandts showed little respect for aura of the forest's grandeur. Instead they delighted in the unsavoury side that industry has foisted on the virgin land. They seized on what surrounds them, operating in the same terrain as folk artists. There is an apparent similarity to naive or folk art but their appropriative stance separates them from outsider art. Rustic furniture is a good example of folk art which the Brandts turn to their own ends. The rustic furniture tradition has considerable status in the craft world today. Bark, twig, branch – those are the worthy relics of the tree. Craig Gilborn closes his 'Introduction' to *Adirondack Furniture and the Rustic Tradition* on this romantic note:

> Rustic is cunning, like Halloween masks and costumes, and the shuddering it evokes is part real and part play. Branch, twig, and root are visible tokens of a domain outside human society. Just as Nature abhors a vacuum, so does it ...abhor the straight line and symmetry that are contrivances of the mind....Today's revival of interest in rustic work may be more than passing fancy, but rather a response under our technological skins to an age-old belief that trees really are occupied by god or spirits. We may be druids at heart.[5]

The Brandts recycled the rustic tradition in *Adirondackland* to highlight the tree's byproducts – newspaper, waferboard – and they commemorated the ultimate eyesore – the stump. They made over the rustic into artifacts that other locals use, memorialise and sell in their front yards. In copying the rustic, they access a spectrum of cultural production equated with leisure, wealth and good living. Their souvenir trinkets made of authentic, cheap materials challenge the standards of high craft which accentuate expensive, often precious materials. It is true that many craft artists do use the idiosyncratic, even the tawdry and cheap; however, when they select the plebeian, they transfigure it into the orderly and formally pleasing. While this is equally true of the Brandts' craft objects, the merchandise in the *Adirondackland* shop broadcast its commodified status. The stock disavowed the standards of fine craft in favour of the souvenir.

The other site in *Adirondackland* was a clearing in the woods, a respite with many uses. It referred historically to the Adirondack camp. These camps functioned in two ways. They were male enclaves, getaways to hunt and fish with the assistance of the able guide. They were also second homes, escapes for the wealthy from the city. In either rendition, rustic-styled objects and furniture were prized. Rustic birch furniture is widely disseminated as signifier of the outdoors and vacationland. This is particularly true in the Northeast, but the style of the rustic is recognisable anywhere.

In the past, ownership of nature's pristine retreat privileged the wealthy, but today's tourist is likely to be a weekend hiker-canoeist-camper – one espousing conservation and preservation. Today's environmentally conscious recreationist was one user of *Adirondackland*'s clearing in the woods. But this clearing was the province of hunters and loggers as well. This space, if actually shared, would likely provoke hostilities. At the centre of the tableau was a dimly lit campfire (red cellophane in front of a rotating light bulb) rising from the centre of a large truck tyre. The walls of the gallery were covered with camouflage, appropriate gear for the hunter. This camouflage, however, was strikingly different. The Brandts jigsawed together typical Park images: a deer trophy head, a lumberjack, a chainsaw, an Adirondack chair. The abstract shapes in standard camouflage converge muted colours and shapes into a surface that masks structure. The Brandts' camouflage, however, created recognisable images of blended khaki greens and brown which registered as form and content. In nature, as in culture, camouflage works to shield the moving predator or victim. Conversely, it conceals the stationary predator or victim in hiding. Camouflage works through confusing background, middle ground, and foreground. This property of camouflage is pivotal in Susie Brandt's textiles and the installations.

In the clearing in *Adirondackland*, as in the larger landscape, humans not only shared this place but left particular footprints. Here the detritus reinforced this multiple use. The hunter stopped here. Evidence of target practice remained – a discarded TV sits atop a bullet-riddled metal drum. The urban camper stopped by, leaving a plastic Perrier sun umbrella. Perhaps the most uncomfortable occupants would have been the tired hikers looking for a peaceful spot to pitch their tents. But this clearing was not only for campers, even this mixed set. The chainsaws installed on stumps were brazenly aggressive – the logger also asserted rights to this spot of earth. Recreational spot, logging header,[6] wilderness – how can all these exist together?

The reality is that they do. The web of attitudes created by the varied population is the core of *Adirondackland's* organisation as museum display. Theoretical and historical attitudes about the American land and American craft reveal themselves. They bind together three strains: the destruction of the forest (quintessential example of land use in America), the conflict between private and public property, and the history of craft and how it has been perceived. The various occupants of Susie Brandt's tableaux do not comprise a compatible version of American life. *Adirondackland* celebrates an aesthetic governed by the vernacular. The quotidian is often outside the mainstream of belief in American pastoralism and acceptable land use. Moreover, in its sly humour which punctures pretensions to humility and the earthy, Susie Brandt's aesthetic stands outside that of the mainstream of American craft.

Spirituality and American Craft

Art and, even more so, craft have been reluctant to admit a variety of life styles with differing political beliefs based on economics and geography. If the clearing in the forest is the place where civilisation enters, this sacred place has been reserved for a particular kind of individual – one who reveres nature. The clearing is a hiatus; it is within or next to the forest but outside the myths that surround it. In the myth, trees are sacred beings and the forest itself is divine. An early painting from the Hudson River School[7] is one of the most famous: Asher Durand's *Kindred Spirits* (1835). The scene depicts Thomas Cole, one of the first painters in this school, standing with his palette and maulstick. He is conversing with William Cullen Bryant, a poet of like-minded transcendental enthusiasm. Cole expressed his sentiments and fears for the forest in a letter he wrote to his patron Luman Reed: 'they are cutting down all the trees in the beautiful valley on which I have looked so often with a loving eye. This throws quite a gloom over my spring anticipations. Tell this to Durand – not that I wish to give him pain, but that I want him to join with me in maledictions on all dollar-godded utilitarians'.[8] This is the quintessential belief in the divine forest, here expressed in the nineteenth century but commonly held today.

Mary Douglas, in her 1995 monograph, *The Craftsman as Yeoman: Myth and Cultural Identity in American Craft*, traced the emergence and triumph of the idyllic and romantic in American craft. Her revisionist stance specified the bond of crafts and nature forged both by the makers and by the press. Douglas observed that where the artist lives is essential to his/her identity. The romance of the woods or the allure of the rural life clings to this ideal. Until recently the role of craftsman in the United States has been that of the modest visionary. The craftsperson's house on a few rural acres defines the craftsperson as well as the work produced. The craftsperson believes making beautiful and satisfying things is possible becauses s/he has created the ideal place to make it happen. A spirituality grounded in nature is embedded in twentieth-century craft. While this is only part of the picture, it is a myth that informs the story of American craft. The city, machines and technology exert a strong pull, but the ideal of the simple life on the land forms the mystique of craft – marking this life as special and different. The studio craft movement, emerging in the 1970s, continues to enforce this aesthetic and succeeds largely because it controls the display and marketing of this particular brand of craft objects.

The earliest phase of the craft model is the village smithy. This ideal was carried forward into the twentieth century where it was embedded in the Arts and Crafts movement. Another chapter began when World War II veterans were demobilised from the army. Granted a college education by the GI Bill, they flocked to burgeoning art schools. These students, predominantly men, reacting to the upheaval of war, believed that the immediacy of working with one's hands was necessary in order to centre oneself. The peace needed to create could best be achieved away from the city, away from the seat of academia and the business world.

The craftsman and place are bonded through proprietary care. This is consonant with the Jeffersonian agrarian model. This ideal is the basis of the myth that Mary Douglas unveiled using examples from several craft magazines, including *American Craft Magazine*. Douglas identified articles written in the late 1970s and early 1980s which described the craftperson's link to the land. Photographs within the article worked to substantiate this, often by positioning the objects in pastoral settings. Photos in gallery advertisements fostered this same mystique. Land is sacred. In this predominantly male world, the stars were potters, woodworkers, glassblowers and metalsmiths. Livelihood depends on self-sustenance. Citing a 1983 *American Craft* article on David Shaner, a potter and rancher in Big Fork, Montana, Douglas pointed out a pair of photographs, one above the other. The top photo showed a profile shot of the craftsman wearing a rancher's jacket and gazing left, or west, eyes trained on the distant horizon. Rolling hills dominate the lower photo; in the middle ground stretches a windbreak of trees, and in the distance the mountains rise. The caption coupled maker with the land: 'His ceramics are rooted in a loving attention to the natural world'.[9]

Two influences, transcendentalism and Zen Buddhism, converged to create what Douglas called a mythopoetic stance. The historical precedent of transcendentalism in the philosophies of Ralph Waldo Emerson and Henry

David Thoreau, merged with contemporary craft practice, heavily influenced by Zen Buddhism, especially in ceramics, as seen in the examples of Bernard Leach, Shoji Hamada, and Soetu Yanagi, founder of Mingei, the Japanese folkcraft movement.[10]

If the mythic landscape is the agrarian ideal, home of the pioneer, its counterpart and often opposite is the mythic landscape of the forest. The forest is in perpetual conflict with the farm. The conflict is historically played out in humanity's fear and affection for the forest coupled with continuous effort not only to tame the forest but to eradicate it. The mythic stature of the forest is not of primary concern to Douglas; her thesis is centred within the agrarian model which posits that ownership of the land is fulfilled through use. This naturally entails the destruction of the forest. The point and counterpoint of this saga is, however, an important chapter in the way Americans view the land. It is also relevant to the primacy of place in Susie Brandt's work, the way she is informed by the landscape, and the relationship of the forest to the politics and economics of its landscape.

Any locale in the USA contains many realities, prodigious amounts of stuff, many ways of making a living. Preservation may or may not be a priority in these locales, but in Adirondack Park it is a high priority where the ideal of the forest is linked to the wilderness. Adirondack Park is an American wilderness dream and misadventure. Once forested mountains, it has, like most forests, been cleared for farms or logged for timber and replanted or simply regrown several times over. While the west retains the aura of wilderness that was once American frontier, the forests of the east may actually be more complex because they record several more generations of human intercourse with the land. The forest and the city are in closer proximity. Adirondack Park reflects the spectrum of the land and land use values.

Every site holds the trace of its previous occupant. Most sites, then, are contested. The history of craft is a contested site as well. It pits the natural against the made, the organic against the constructed, and poses the conundrum – is it hand and mind or mind and hand? The romance of nature and the human desire for self-reliance and separation from the social contract suggests that everything worthy can be found away from the city. It can be shaped into its purest form using simple tools. Conversely, the machine, civilisation's fruit, makes possible excellent as well as efficient production. Because craft is so firmly implicated in the myth of a natural world, the benefits of the machine are always equivocal and must be justified. While William Morris admired and used the newest in textile machinery, his praise was never without the admonition of the corrupting power that machines bring about in the lives of men and women.

The bucolic vision of a few sheep, a spinning wheel and a handloom fits the description of the agrarian idyll that Mary Douglas gives us. Yet this way of life through crafts never produced the aura for textiles that it did in clay, glass or metal. Most of the heroes of American craft who came to fame in the 1970s cited by Douglas are male. It is hardly necessary to mention that textile handcrafts in the Western world have been primarily the domain of women. Industrialised machinery in textiles has a long shadow. The machine as the production tool has influenced fibre arts / textiles more than other media in the handcraft movement, as the example of Anni Albers at the Bauhaus demonstrates.

The machine is interloper. It operates in a middle ground where it creates new possibilities for humans while disrupting the environment. The metaphorical dimension of middle ground is significant as a key to the perception of craft and the part that the machine, the quotidian and the vernacular have played in that history. Foreground, middle ground, background are familiar descriptors of the space in painting. Often the middle ground in a painting is significant because it is where two extremes co-exist. The middle landscape is actual but it is also metaphorical; it is the place where human interaction enters and begins to change the landscape. An example of this is the mitigation of the idealised agrarian by the introduction of the machine. Leo Marx in *TheMachine in the Garden* provides a veritable roadmap to the art and literature that marks this change. In the nineteenth century the train symbolised energy in motion and was a sign of all that will transpire. Marx said about George Inness's painting:

> *The Lackawanna Valley* (1855) is a striking representation of the idea that machine technology is a proper part of the landscape. Like Thoreau's extended metaphor at the end of *Walden*, the springtime thawing of the sand in the railroad bank, Inness's painting seems to say that 'there is nothing inorganic'. Instead of causing disharmony, the train is a unifying device. The hills in the background and the trees of the middle distance gently envelop the industrial buildings and artifacts. No sharp lines set off the man-made from the natural terrain. Nor is the Lackawanna's smoke unpleasant. The cottony puffs that rise from the engine and the roundhouse are merely duplicates of a puff that rises from behind the church – an ingenious touch! Instead of cutting the space into sharp, rectilinear segment as railroad tracks often do, the right-of-way divides in two, forming the delicately touching ovals that dominate the middle plane.[11]

The machine here is not villain but helpful beast, gratefully accommodated into daily life and made a part of the scene. This is another version of pastoralism, the Jeffersonian ideal that Mary Douglas described. Important too, Inness painted his landscape in 1855 when neither force suppressed the other; the machine offered hope not destruction. Soon thereafter the machine became more and more onerous. In *The Lackawanna Valley*, however, as Marx pointed out, these views were in positive tension.

In Susie Brandt's works the middle ground operates to acknowledge two views of craft – celebration of hand and mind and of mind and machine. The vernacular is present both as material choice and subject matter. An embrace of the vernacular stands in the middle ground, that is, in this corridor between the ideal and the real a non-mythic craft stance emerges. The vernacular provides a non-purist, anti-romantic view of the land. To look at the wilderness evenhandedly means to look at the wilderness as it is transformed by the axe, chainsaw, paper mill, mine, and happy camper.

Landscape architect and writer J. B. Jackson comfortably accepted the ambivalence of mass culture. His writings encircle many life-styles and all kinds of adaptation to the land. He applauded the disdained – the mobile home is a particular object of fascination for Jackson. The concept of wilderness is important, he believed, chiefly as another site of human interaction. In *Beyond Wilderness* Jackson wrote:

> An essential characteristic of the American forest was its privatization, its fragmenting into countless small holdings. As the destruction of the immense common forest proceeded, it became customary for every homestead to reserve a portion – usually a quarter – of the land for a woodlot....a genuine miniature forest, visible on the farm landscape of America until about a half-century ago. That fragmentation, noted even in early colonial times, came about because we lacked any memory of the communal forest, essential in any European landscape, and also of necessity lacked any common historical or mythical memory, holding us all together.[12]

In the Adirondacks, while land was never owned and controlled by a nobility for hunting, large land tracts belonged to the wealthy or logging and mining companies. Much of this acreage has dispersed into smaller holdings. The forest primeval has disappeared, but the supremacy of this ideal hangs on. In Jackson's eyes, to see the wilderness experience as mystical is misleading. One result of the weekend in the wild is that nature takes on the aura of the divine; it reveals that humans, along with all living things, are inseparable

Plate 1
Lorna Jin-gubarangunyja
Dilly Bag
(Manigrida Arts & Culture, Arnhem Land, Northern Territory, Australia)
open weave

Plate 2
Quilted bag
Gujsat (India)
hand-embroidery

Plate 3
Lynn Setterington (GB)
Nine Objects
hand-embroidered quilt
60 x 62cm

Plate 4
Sarbjit Natt (GB/India)
Mughal (1996)
textile dyes and pigment on silk
168 x 110cm
(in the collection of Bradford Art Galleries & Museums)

Plate 5
Fahmida Shah
Untitled (1996)
handpainted silk and textile dyes
209 x 112cm

Plate 6a (above)
Betsy Brandt, Susie Brandt,
Richard Carey (USA)
Water Tower Project (1997)

Plate 6b (below)
Susie Brandt (USA)
After Albers (1998) (detail)
pantyhose, handwoven on potholder loom
l88 x 147cm

Plate 7
Susie Brandt (USA)
Adirondackland (1995)
NYS Biennial, NYS Museum, Albany NY
mixed-media installation, fire ring and tent

Plate 8 & 9
Diana Wood Conroy (Australia)
Unwritten Country with a Fragment of Roman Mosaic (1998)
wool, silk, metal thread
100x250cm

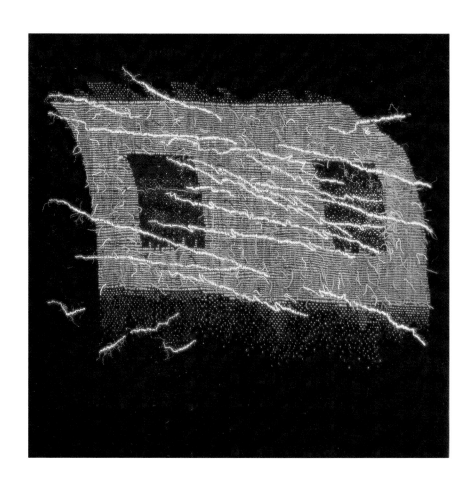

Plate 10
Wlodzimierz Cygan (Poland)
Widziales? (1994)
woven tapestry, wool, polyamide, sisal,
180 x 165cm

Plate 11
Wlodzimierz Cygan
1999 (1998)
woven tapestry, wool, sisal
320 x 350cm

Plate 12
Paola Moreno (Chile)
Atadura Atávica (1996)
printed cloth on cement stands
200 x 170 x 32cm

Plate 13
Yinka Shonibare (GB/Nigeria)
A Victorian Philanthropist's Parlour (1997)
printed fabrics
installation at London Printworks, Brixton

Plate 14
Kai Chan (China/Hong Kong/Canada)
A Walk from A to B (1997)
bamboo
102 x 74 x 27cm

Plate 15
Phoebe Man (Hong Kong)
A Present for her Growth I (1996)
mixed media
300 x 300 x 60cm

Plate 16
Kith Tsang
Hello! Hong Kong – Part 4 (1996)
cloth, bed
installation at Rennie's Mill, Hong Kong

parts of the cosmic order. Yet for all its intensity, it is a temporary thing. We return to the everyday world, though perhaps spiritually transformed. In Jackson's estimation the getaway is fine; the trouble with this experience is that it inspires a distasteful comparison between the primordial natural world and the world most of us linve in.[13] In a larger sense, the wilderness experience itself can be read as camouflage – a protective screen that momentarily disables everyday life.

Camouflage: a Confusion of Boundaries

A metaphorical reading of camouflage connects the Brandts' enterprise to the importance of the vernacular in that it recognises and accepts multiple uses of the land. It carries as well into the terrain of craft seen in the Brandts' situating of the common and scorned as delightful and valued. The Brandts employ camouflage for its textile properties and for its convergence with painting. Primarily, camouflage is disguise through artifice. Artifice is the key operative, for what *Adirondackland* suggests is that nothing is really hidden, but everything is made. There is nothing subversive about camouflage; it is easy to see through it. Camouflage works best when the eye cannot differentiate figure from ground; but, camouflage works only momentarily, fooling the eye until something moves, subject or object. The epitome would be to invent a mask that would work from any point in the landscape. The reality is impossible. But camouflage constructs a valiant attempt, it smudges interfaces between sectors. In painting it is the intersection of foreground, middle ground, background. In warfare it is targets in the landscape. Gertrude Stein recalled Picasso's wondrous realisation:

> I very well remember at the beginning of the war being with Picasso on the Boulevard Raspail when the first camouflaged truck passed. It was at night, we had heard of camouflage but we had not yet seen it and Picasso amazed looked at it and then cried out, yet it is we who made it, that is cubism.[14]

Camouflage's effects can usually be defused. It serves to confuse by interrupting a logical perspectival progression. Furthermore, camouflage reinforces the inexpensive. It is cheap to manufacture and market and it is easy, fast and cheap to construct in the environment.

The camouflage-painted gallery in the clearing tableau in *Adirondackland* is pivotal in another installation, a collaboration of the two Brandt sisters and Richard Carey. *Water Tower Project* (1997) [see colour plate no. 6a] is visually documented fiction; the trio's camouflage paint job exists only in photograph slides. They created a camouflage print and then using Adobe Photoshop, they superimposed the print onto a slide photograph of two large water towers. Taking a cue from their pictorial *Adirondackland* camouflage of deer trophy heads and chainsaws, they composed another camouflage print. For Water Tower Project they abutted yellow, forest green, and aqua stags, trucks, and an outline map in the shape of the Park.

The camouflage print cannot be seen driving along the Interstate 87 where the water towers are a prominent landmark at Exit 19 near Glens Falls, but the location is significant. Locale once again describes land use, as these water towers are just inside the southern boundary of Adirondack Park. Fictional reality in *Water Tower Project* is a replay of the myth of the sacred forest, a place of heightened vision which holds an illusory, awesome possibility. Yet it is the myth debunked in the familiar Brandt brand of camouflage. In the slide the water towers are still obvious; neither their form nor function is convincingly disguised. *Water Tower Project* may provide a mask, but it does not hide the water towers any more than the blue-green paint on the actual towers hides them. Is this colour of ficial 'water tower colour'? And does it stem from a desire to camouflage? The colour little resembles the sky; it does little to blend water towers into the landscape. Maybe colour pickers choose a 'pleasing' colour that will help water towers be overlooked in their surroundings. The computer-assisted camouflage job makes the landmark neither less nor more noticeable. Camouflage appears in many guises, but it is as ubiquitous textile mode that it suits Brandt's methodology. The ultimate military commodity, camouflage stands out in store-front windows across America, purporting to disguise but instead asserting its presence.

Camouflage certifies that it is artifacture that makes evident this perceptual phenomen. Does it matter that reality is simulated through the computer? Is this art or simply a visual pun available only to cognoscenti who see the slide? A few years ago this question might have stirred debate but no longer. Virtual reality is now part of the art landscape.

The Brandts/Carey collaboration in Photoshop partakes in the acceptance of new technology. More than acceptance, this embrace of the promise of the new is an essential component of modernism and even of one brand of American pastoralism as seen in Leo Marx's reading of George Inness's *Lackawanna Valley*. The Brandts/Carey camouflage job accepts mediation in landscape and recognizes that removal is not the answer. This 'solution' echoes J. B. Jackson's pluralistic stance.

Finally, *Water Tower Project's* reliance on technology echoes Albers and her Bauhaus belief in coupling the hand with the machine using material as the bridge. Material is central to Albers philosophy and methodology. Mary Jane Jacobs names Albers's 'concept of material as a culturally guiding force.'[15] Brandt, like Albers, is voracious in her search and acceptance of unusual materials. However, there are limits. Neither artist steps into the territory of the transgresive and both depend on order according to textile formats and standards of craftsmanship. The materials that Brandt gathers are slightly more uncomfortable than in Albers's necklaces made of 'household and hardware items: curtain rings, hairpins, paper clips, bottle caps, glass drawer knobs, clay insulators, metal washers, gilt door springs, and angel braces, some of which were strung of door chains'.[16] This is largely the result of contemporary art's wholesale adoption of the quotidian as the motherlode. Susie Brandt, like Albers, assigns high status to material. Equally important is her emphasis on textile production. The invented cloth of both artists carries the meaning of its individual constituents and remakes the units into a composite that is a mappa mundi.

Notes

1.   Mary Douglas, *The Craftsman as Yeoman: Myth and Cultural Identity in American Craft*, Haystack Monograph series, Deer Isle, ME, 1995.

2.   Mary Jane Jacobs, 'Anni Albers: A Modern Weaver as Artist,' *The Woven and Graphic Art of Anni Albers*, Smithsonian Press, Washington, D.C., 1985, pp. 68, 67.

3.   Although she presently teaches at University of the Arts, Philadelphia, Pennsylvania, Brandt also lives in her hometown, Corinth, a small town within the boundaries of the Adirondack Park.

4.   Lucy Lippard, 'Looking Around: Where We Are, Where We Could Be,' *Mapping the Terrain: New Genre Public Art*, (ed. Lucy Lippard), Bay Press, Seattle, WA,1995, p. 114.

5.   Craig Gilborn, *Adirondack Furniture and the Rustic Tradition*, Harry N. Abrams, New York, 1987, p. 18.

6.   A logging header is the site where the cut trees are massed for shipment to lumber mills.

7.   The Hudson River flows through Adirondack Park. The Hudson River School of Painting, however, is associated with a more southerly portion of the river between Albany and New York City.

8.   Barbara Novak, *Nature and Culture*, Oxford University Press, New York, 1980, p. 164.

9.   *ibid.*,p. 3.

10.   Douglas, *op. cit.*, p. 4.

11.   Leo Marx, *The Machine in the Garden*, Oxford University Press, New York, 1967, pp. 220-221.

12 .   J. B. Jackson, *A Sense of Place, a Sense of Time*, Yale University Press, New Haven,1994, p. 83.

13.   *ibid.*, p. 87.

14.   Gertrude Stein, Picasso, Beacon Press, Boston, 1959, p. 11.

15.   Jacobs, *op. cit.*, p. 69.

16.   *ibid.*, p. 68.

*   Publisher's note: a 48 page monograph of the work of Susie Brandt, publ. 2004 by Telos, is available from www.arttextiles.com

A DEEPER EXAMINATION

Wlodzimierz Cygan

Textile art exists on the edge. That is what gives it its character as an art medium. It lives on the fringes of so many everyday human activities. It is adjacent to so much. Our spoken language, for example, has appropriated countless images from the textile world: we talk of the rich tapestry of life, or of the fabric of our society. I can think of no other creative medium that is so intimately enmeshed with our day-to-day lives.

I am thinking of the process of making, just as much as of the finished piece of textile art. There is something so natural about tapestry weaving, for example, that reminds me of walking. I have known how to walk ever since my first memories of life. Some of my best ideas have come to me when walking.

Despite the fact that for centuries our human language has remained reasonably consistent, we nonetheless endeavour repeatedly to create an individual and unique form for our verbal messages. And so it is with our fibre art: I continue to harbour the illusion that nobody has ever woven quite the way I do.

Some of my works satisfy my quest for uniqueness. I am up to date with specialist literature, exhibition catalogues, art magazines. I take part in numerous exhibitions and artists' symposia, whether in an active or passive capacity. And I confess that I derive great pleasure from the fact that most of my own methods and solutions are not used elsewhere by others!

The Artists' Work

In order to avoid copying another's work, or in order to avoid repeating oneself, some artists consider it best to search out something new, to undertake a rapid journey toward lands as yet undiscovered. Others instead prefer to concentrate on their immediate reality, on a deeper penetration and examination of their own domain. By 'deeper' I am not referring to the 'meaning' or 'messages' carried by one's art. It should not matter whether the threads are green, white or black, nor whether the image is painted, photographed or computed, unless there is some link between the structure of the fabric and the image it carries. Instead, the integrity and purposefulness of one's *atelier* can constitute value in its own right, and in the eyes of observers. For an artist, an ongoing process of deeper penetration or examination involves a renewed willingness to discover and trace numerous possibilities, thus establishing new qualities or links in the creative process.

This deeper examination that goes on in the studio is akin to the work of a scientist, who conducts minute and meticulous observations, careful

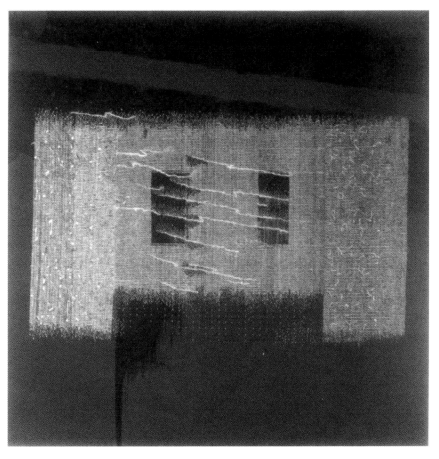

Wlodzimierz Cygan
Headquarters (1997) (detail)
woven tapestry, woollen fibre, sisal
240 x 250cm

not to omit any phase which might have a bearing on his core research. A breakthrough may come about as a result of the sudden realisation of an unexpected link between two areas which had previously been thought unconnected. The individual pieces of information themselves have not changed, but their value has been transformed, and they now become a key with which to open doors to areas previously shut off.

If we work without penetrating more deeply, we are in danger of overexploiting the same narrow repertoire of expectations. We should be willing to extend our scope of research. This can happen in a sense spontaneously, as soon as we realise that life can never be brought to a standstill, nothing is ever as it was before. Not only have we developed as individuals, but so too have science and communications developed, and of course the access to new materials and technologies has taken great leaps forward. It is worth scrutinising earlier art in the light of new attainments. In studying group exhibition catalogues from the past we can clearly see what has survived the test of time, and what is no longer – or maybe never was – of value.

An artist's inquiry into permanent values can be understood as a personal pilgrimage toward perfection. One of my colleagues at the Gdansk Academy of Fine Arts, Jacek Friedrich, expressed it thus:

> I understand perfection as consisting of 'development within tradition'. Developing within a tradition is like climbing higher and higher up the rungs of a ladder. But an alternate way, the way of novelty and innovation, is to leap from one ladder to another like an acrobat: never mind whether you land on a higher or lower rung, you are always landing somewhere new.
>
> Now, both tactics have their advantages and disadvantages, and I am not saying that one is better than the other. They each offer their own vantage points for observation. What is interesting is the neverending polarity of the two approaches: despite centuries of attempts to harmonise them, they remain as different as ever. Perhaps it is this underlying tension that makes art so endlessly fascinating. Perhaps settling the argument would lead to the withering of art.*-

The need for perfection is a personal one. It proceeds from both the conscious choices of a given artist as well as from his or her predispositions and psychological make-up. Ideally, all factors should remain in harmony with

* J. Friedrich, 'On the Education of an Artist', *Text i Textil* no. 21/22 1998, Poland.

one another, in order to achieve the phenomenon of beauty accompanied by truth.

My Starting Point

My starting point is the simple interweave of warp and weft. From here I seek an original way forward into textile art. After so many centuries of technological development it may sound implausible that there could still be anything new out there of any value. I believe there is. The mechanical loom, which has been modernised many times, has not yet managed to overcome the formal limitations imposed by the parallel, single-plane system of warp threads. So there are only very limited possibilities of constructing the textile fabric by means of manipulating the warp. This constitutes the skeleton on which a tapestry is constructed. The skeleton tells us most explicitly about the fundamental structure of a given organism.

I have abandoned the loom in favour of the frame, in order not to feel so restrained. Sometimes I try to invent and construct simple devices which let me form my warp freely. Through a conscious selection of material and colour they can still form *additionally* – and I must stress this word – an image on the constructed textile. I believe that the fabric is the core of the textile work, not the image rendered on it, the image of some other reality. The coloured threads on the skeleton are only an added quality which could perhaps find better expression in another technique.

Recent Work

My work entitled '1999' [see colour plate no. 11] sums up my recent preoccupations. On an emotional level, I feel a sense of wonder combined with an irrational fear and apprehension as we approach the end of our century. What bothers me is the combination of high technology together with the chaotic, haphazard tangle of much of our world. The form of '1999' refers to a monumental clock face. Despite the absence of numbers or hands, it nonetheless suggests the dynamic, never-ending revolutions of time. I try to express the abstraction of the notion of time through the paradoxical form of a square circle or the round square. The technique I applied is that of stretching the warp and weft around the circle. This work has a form and technique which I have used before, but here I am particularly pleased at their purposeful application.

'ALL ORNAMENTS ARE USEFUL TO SCALE FAÇADES'

Julián Ruesga Bono
(translated by Paula Larkin)

Order of knowledge is based on exclusion, the task is to expose (include?) these exclusions.
Michel Foucault

Within Western artistic culture, textiles are considered as secondary and marginal elements, relegated to the category of the lavish, the popular and the functional, far from the sublime expressive level in which our culture catalogues what we call art. However, precisely because of that, many artists are working from within the textile category, within its functional and social usage, as a critical form for rethinking culture and its relation to power and hierarchy. This essay is a reflection on that theme and, in particular, on the situation of national cultures whose development differs from countries where the impetus of modernity is in strong evidence.

Choosing a Building

Modernisation is a process in which all vital, intellectual and social circumstances were radically revolutionised. The process slowly disconnected art in Europe from the social and cultural functions it had in the past.

Until the end of the Middle Ages artists carried out work commissioned by ecclesiastic authorities, adopting symbolic and figurative codes that they were obliged to reproduce without any pretensions of originality. During the Classic era, artists' work was subordinated to the guidelines of the courts and the changes wrought by war and peace. The growth of capitalism from the 16th and 17th centuries facilitated the bourgeois cultural liberalisation, so that religious and courtly guardianship became weaker, disintegrating little by little. Members of the aristocracy began mixing with lay-intellectuals and a special market emerged for artistic activities.

As a result, the artistic field was formed with relative independence and its own internal criteria of legitimacy. The progressive complexity of the productive process within the new capitalist context made for differentiation in areas of work, separation in such aspects of human activities as culture, politics, economics and daily life, and thus each one was progressively liberated. The bourgeois public made possible the existence of a specific market for cultural objects, in which works were chosen and valued with aesthetic criteria, giving the artists a hitherto unknown independence in their choice of themes and forms. Thus, during the 18th century, literature, fine arts and music became institutionalised as independent activities, gaining a higher degree of autonomy in definition of both space and practice. The distance between the culture of experts and that of the public at large grew wider. Now accorded specialised treatment and reflection, art did not necessarily pass into daily praxis.

Nevertheless, within capitalism art objects were converted into merchandise. Along with the appearance of an autonomous art market came the need for places to exhibit the merchandise, places where the works could be seen and bought: museums and galleries. Painters abandoned their big walls and

Consuelo Jimenez Underwood
Banderas de la Frontera (1993) (detail)
printed textile, barbed wire
127 x 213 x 6cm

reduced their space to canvas, which furthermore was enclosed in a frame; sculptors no longer tried to adapt their work to the proportions of a public space, but instead were limited by the autonomous requirements of exhibition and private locations; tapestry became smaller and, as with painting and sculpture, progressively substituted the biographical illustrations of saints, evangelical quotes and military gestures of the monarchs for exotic scenes of interest to the emerging bourgeois of the 18th century.

Finally, during the 19th century an aesthetic conception appeared that stimulated artists to produce their work according to the concept of art for art's sake. Thus, the artists could give personal expression to the experiences encountered in their own activities; they could create outside the obligations of routine knowledge and daily action. Art became a self-sufficient activity based on impartial contemplation and directed towards the production of very specialised aesthetic-symbolic messages. As artistic movements erased or reduced the naturalist references that previously had maintained the illusion of reality, and imposed specific research in relation to the autonomous demands of the artists' profession, the distance between creation and comprehension grew. While demanding an audience which was well-informed in the dynamics of the aesthetic field, the artists' activity withdrew mainly to specialised areas.

From the historical point of view, when art became autonomous from the patronage system and thereby became 'art' in the modern sense, then the institutions of art emerged, regulating the artistic cultural field. Museums, galleries, art critics, markets, schools and even the guilds, slowly began to form the artistic institution, generating the dominant ideas that involved, to a great extent, the public's sensitivity, as well as the artistic condition. Art as an institution established itself with ideal values. These values were represented as those of the emerging bourgeois class which identified its rising ambitions and the importance of respectability with the break away from all that was associated with the disowned universe. Bourgeois values proposed a means of legitimising and securing economic power through the accumulation of symbolic capital. In this process, art was sustained in its independence from the old social order.

Art was to be self-sufficient, the expression of the artist's individual inventiveness and his/her creative capacity. Art was expected to adapt itself to society's constant progess. Art's typical customers represented a specific class who directed, controlled and orchestrated culture in relation to their own values, objectives and the social structure they generated.

The art institution, as an elitist space, no longer included other practices considered less noble, more pragmatic and functional, incapable of eliminating their practical side. Manual trades and craftsmanship were considered uncouth and backward, and relegated to an outside place and devalued. Popular cultural practices, too, were defined and devalued, even by the marginal sectors themselves. There was continual reference to the dominant aesthetic, that is to say the aesthetic of those who knew how to differentiate real art, art that could be admired within the liberty and impartiality of sublime taste.

Planning an Ascent

The autonomy of art – which was never absolute and depended on the market and its variations of interest – created the illusion that the aesthetic field is indifferent to social pressure, that the works transcend history and are always available to be enjoyed, like a language with no barriers, for people from any era, nation or social class. An 'essence of art' was assumed to be beyond the variations through which it expressed itself.

Our conceptual structures, those with which we created and legitimised the different orders in which culture is formed, have been altered by a growing complexity. Nowadays we problematise the mistaken ties with traditions that we sought to exclude or surpass in or er to establish cultural hegemony. We aspire to a more open manner of thinking, capable of interaction and integration between different levels, classes and forms of collective sensitivity. It hasn't escaped our notice that cultural projects and their social staging are going through a change which nurtures a new sensitivity and goes beyond the rhetoric which functions to legitimise structures of power. The partiality of art and the hierarchial order of culture has been exposed by theoretical studies and research on the relationships between the social order and production of the imaginary.

In this process, it has become clear that cultural analysis itself may be predetermined by social order and the ideology by which it is sustained. The theory and history of art are challenged to acknowledge the conditioning that derives from the production, circulation and consumption of artistic goods. The object of aesthetics and art history cannot be the artwork alone: these disciplines must investigate also the process of production and social circulation in which its meanings are established and modified.

In fact, the attempt to sever the connection between art and cultural hegemony is not new. Throughout the 20th century, different *avant-garde* movements tried to modify the effects ot artistic practice on the social scene, attempting to transcend the elitist solitude of art for art's sake. Here the artistic *avant-garde* becomes interesting because of the ruptures it often caused in the social order of artistic production, its acts of sabotage, and its capacity for destruction of art as an institution. The *avant-garde* represented creative liberalisation, but not merely as a machine of change or stylistic regeneration of artistic forms. Like theoretical investigations, the artistic practices of these *avant-garde* movements tried, at various times and by various means, to take apart and overthrow the established codes, to criticise art both in its function as merchandise and as a reproduction of moral conventions. Above all, they sought to open it up to new ways of thinking and perceiving art, outside that which was institutionalised by the hegemonic culture. The artistic *avant-garde* (Dadá, Surrealism, Futurism, Russian *avant-garde*, Situationists) was characterised by an iconoclastic attitude and a critical inquiry into the ontological status of art in modern society. What interests us is that they sought to demystify and undermine the legitimising discourse of elitist art in Western society and its pretensions of aesthetic knowledge.

Do not misinterpret me – I am not saying that our thinking about art today is the same as that of the historical *avant-gardes*. But they do share a critical attitude that, together with the changed social context, has given art another point of view, another reading, and has created favourable circumstances for an altered sensibility.

The depth of this change is still only skin-deep in most areas, especially those which base their privileged hegemonic position in old cultural structures. But, in an ever-increasing sector of our culture, we are witnessing a clear transformation in the sensitivity with which theories and practices are formed. These theories and practices not only differ from the hegemonic discourse but also position themselves in the opposite field as another way of understanding culture and life. It is no longer credible to idealise the artist as a genius whose works are sanctified and exalted; nor is it credible to attribute these qualities to inspiration or mysterious virtues. Today we think of the artistic subject, as we would of any other, as the result of collective structures, in which relationships, cultures and economics intersect. If we want to talk about the artist, then the concept must be worked out anew to rid it of egocentric illusions and make it capable of designating a conditioned and creative subject.

Equally, art is the product of a series of interferences, traditions and innovations, lectures and texts, and cultural constructions. It is within its public circulation that it begins to gain meaning and sense, becoming enriched with the attention and imagination of those who receive it, altering its meaning depending on the different classes and societies within which it is viewed. From this perspective, art is as much use as it is instrument. A work of art begins to exist when it is in contact with the world from which it proceeds and to which it returns. It reveals the paradoxical multiplicity of the world, the ambiguity and uncertainty. Art needs these elements of multiplicity, ambiguity and uncertainty to subsist and exist, and to structure the act of thinking as a constructive display of meaning.

In art we find the artist and the spectator, the place and the technology, the social and the individual, production and distribution, singularity and multiplicity, the true and the false, politics and economics, the norm and dissidence, museums and academies, and the outside references and the internal phantoms. That is to say, we end up finding a great deal of ourselves in as much as we are producers of meaning, or story builders cloaked with a certain existential complexity. To understand the phenomenon and concept of art one must go through the process of acknowledging the complexity of human existence, and the inclusion of art in the various mechanisms of the world.

The Ascent

Social order and the principle of power are legitimised by seemingly transcendental values and unifying ethics. Order and the hegemonic cultural discourse of modernity has been based on a technological vision of progress and an egocentric vision of geography, society, culture and economics. In political terms, opposition to this cultural hegemony has provoked the problematics of 'alternance' in conjunction with the appearance of the 'other', those persons and practices who were excluded from modernity's vision of progress and subordinated to its interests.

Numerous and diverse types of 'alternance' are formed by differences in subjectivity, gender and sexual preferences, race and social class, time and geographical location and migration. Now the exclusion of these subjects is made problematic and their presence as effective subjects on the social scene is vindicated. The 'other' has emerged in contemporary society, and is affirmed through its radical cultural, ethnic, linguistic, sexual, temporal and geographical particularity. We are increasingly obliged to accept a more decentralised, complex and tolerant point of view. We now live in a laboratory of ethical positions, in which the parameters of our political, cultural, historical and aesthetic models are rethought. In general terms, what we call postmodernity is the result of the conjunction of all these and many other processes of confrontations. Postmodernity is a space that is loaded with questions about the conditions under which we build the world.

In this context, it has been precisely women and artists belonging to minority groups who have given a new dimension to cultural critics. Their artistic practice and critical reflection has retrieved hidden and crippled traditions. Their explorations of subjectivity based on gender, sexual preference and race, their aesthetic productions and the debate on social and individual constructions of identity and difference have allowed cultural manifestations, alternative to the hegemonic model, to surface.

There are a great many and a great variety of people living 'Western' culture fluidly and 'incorrectly' in their own way, questioning the established cultural order through artistic practice which is both critical and political. These artists look to local popular culture and imagery to root their work in the tensions and conflicts of contemporary society. They question such issues as racial integration, the role of minorities, consumerism, AIDS, sexual equality, ethical defence of social sectors, and the coexistence of different temporalities. In doing so, they participate in the artistic activism directed at empowering a new cultural paradigm outside the norm. The feminist movement brought many significant changes to the social structure and cultural attitudes. Today, the way in which we raise questions related to gender and sexual preference, to subjectivity and representation, would be unthinkable without the critical impact of feminist discourse. This critical discourse strives to respond to the notion of 'otherness', to the idea of the 'other' as a fundamental concept in philosophy and in psychoanalysis. The theory of Language has used the concept of 'otherness' to critique and revise Language formations which give priority to things masculine, leaving women situated in the place of a non-subject.

Beyond folkloric exoticism, the critical emergence of 'otherness' has entailed the re-evaluation and inclusion of peripheral and secondary cultural models, considered marginal by the elitist culture. Local traditions, pre-modern artistic forms of expression, non-Western cultures and ways of life have been revalued as part of the growing consciousness that other cultures should be known by different means than those of conquest and dominion.

The progressive globalisation of European industrial capitalism from the end of the 18th century, along with its colonial and neo-colonial activities, extended Western culture as the metaculture of modernity around which it linked together the institutions and general functions of daily life. The concept of imperialism became tied up with the phenomena of expansion and economic exploitation, but moreover, its fundamental consequences were related to the very idea of civilisation and culture. From the colonised perspective, colonialism brought the dissolution of regional and local identities that bound the territory to its local history and established the continuity of a complex historical consciousness. For these pre-industrial societies, imperialism meant a social restructuring in which the community's cultural integration no longer rested with historical memory or the human relationship with nature and the ways of thinking linked to traditions. In their place was the supposition that bound ethic values to the functionality of social structures, and these to the governing principle of economic production.

But, like all homogenisation processes on a grand scale, even when one manages to level out the differences, other new ones are generated within themselves. This can be seen both in the re-adaptation of the dominant culture happening in the peripheries and also in the heterogenisation that immigrants are now producing in contemporary metropolis. Culture is established in this way in a field of tensions. A struggle is taking place between hegemonic and secondary social forces, and the ethno-cultural debate is transformed into a political space for power struggles, of both a symbolic and a social nature. In this space other forms of subjectivity are re-affirmed, determined by new social actors who are no longer exclusively white, Western and male.

Many countries, such as Spain, Portugal and Greece, have recently joined up with modernity. Others are doing so without having gone through a process of socio-economic modernisation: the countries from the so-called Third World, noting the heterogenity that this term designates. We could speak of a peripheral modernity where multiple and unequal logics of development cohabit, subordinating national economic elitism, where modernity and the unequal socio-economic modernisation are reduced to the big metropolis while huge populations in rural zones remain excluded.

In these countries modernisation has not worked by substituting the new for the old and the traditional. There were ruptures provoked by industrial development and the accelerated urbanisation of large cities, but the traditional cultures continued carrying out their functions and developing in rural zones far away from the metropolis and the city suburbs. Industrialisation did not cause the disappearance of crafts nor did scientific thinking substitute for myth; they kept on functioning side by side. Traditions and folklore have continued carrying out their social role amongst the masses alongside the new means of communication. Many artisans keep working because their products are still functional and they continue to satisfy traditional demands. In many instances, their contact with the modern side has brought new developments.

In the plastic arts and in writing too, we find signs of inadequacy between modernisation and the local culture of these countries. In the 1920s, modern art was promoted by artists who returned to their countries of origin from Europe. New art was not only brought about by directly transplanted influences, but also by the artists' own responses as they sought ways to make their international experiences compatible with the culture of developing societies which retained a strong sense of everything popular and traditional. For example, the poetry of Garcia Lorca in Spain, Torres García's southern school in Uruguay, and the muralish school in Mexico all represented local themes, placing them within modern aesthetic developments to establish a new art that re-integrated the popular and the learned. One could multiply the examples within contemporary art in African, Asian, American and European countries.

Enjoying the Ascent

The institutionalised idea of art implies a division, a separation, between the (superior) spiritual aesthetic level and the other (inferior) merely pragmatic level. The opposition between the learned and the popular, the modern and the traditional, becomes more intense within the opposition established by the hegemonic aesthetic discourse of art and craft. If one looks on art as an impartial symbolic movement, a set of 'sublime' and 'intellectual' goods, where form predominates over function and beauty over usefulness, then crafts appear as the 'other', the 'peripheral' – a stratum of objects anchored in popular tradition that can never leave behind their practical origins. The development of industry and urban life gave rise to the existence of mass society and the appearance of a great demand for aesthetic consumerism which supposed the denial of this division.

We are witnessing a profound aesthetisation of the social space. The exceptionality and unrepeatability of the works, which legitimated art's claim to eternity, have given way to the mass-production of aesthetic objects. At the same time, the uncertainty and brevity of functional goods has now become part of the aesthetic framework. Thanks to technology, the prototype is opposed to the unrepeatable work within a wider concept of aesthetics. Thus, the old division becomes even more problematic. One could ask, which has more aesthetic force – any example of industrial design seen on the streets every day such as a new car, or the ancient traditional forms of art that have been in existence for aeons? Which has more communicative power – advertising's hyperaesthetised language or the institutionalised language of art? We live in a period when learned art tends no longer to occupy the privileged social place where the aesthetic experience was manifest.

Up until recently we thought we knew what we were talking about when we discussed the popular or the urban. The popular is usually associated with the pre-modern and the subsidiary – maintaining its own forms of production and ways of reproducing local culture, thanks to the survival of pre-industrial enclaves. But traditional popular culture, like elitist culture, is not just a set of objects; it is also social practices and processes of communication. It is a store of a group's previous experiences of coming up with solutions and connecting with its surroundings. The popular, while considered the opposite to the learned or bourgeois culture, meant the common people, that is to say 'the other' of elitist culture, 'the other' of industry, 'the other' of civilisation. At the same time, the urban was the opposite of the rural. The urban was included in the modern and the rural in the traditional. These dichotomies resulted in the creation of boundaries for certain practices and processes that the social experience of recent years has dissolved. Multiple migrations to the cities, both within the one country and from other countries, have radically transformed the city's outlook.

In addition, two more important factors have redrawn the landscape: commercial exchanges, and the arrival of electronic goods to both rural and urban households. Households are connected daily with modern innovation as well as with the traditional information of other cultures and the heritage of other times. Today we are in the midst of a hybrid process of exile, decentralisation and re-organisation, where any attempt at defining or dassifying runs the risk of exduding what may be the most important and novel social experience of the moment. The masses signify a new way of living out popular culture.

The popular and the learned, caught in the middle of an industrial and mercantile shake-up, a re-organisation of symbolic processes, are creating innovative products and consumer practices in cultural merchandise. I am not for a moment suggesting that the new communication technologies are a substitute for our inheritance from the past and for public interaction. But what I am saying is that they are inter- related in a much broader communicative space, creating a more complex arena and multiplying their efficiency. The arts develop in relation to other arts and crafts. Crafts come and go from town to country and they rub shoulders with the arts. Magazines, books, videos, television and cinema tell the story of one culture and these are exchanged with others. Local cultures lose their exclusive relationship with their own territories and gain in knowledge and communication. The hybrid intercommunication that the mass media promotes leads us to participate intermittently with popular and learned, traditional and modern groups.

Right now, all cultures are borderline, all traditions feed off each other within the half-way framework. The massive redistribution of traditional symbolic merchandise by the mass media has generated more fluid interaction between the learned and the popular, between the traditional and the modern, and has re-organised the links between symbolic systems and groups. The mass media have made possible the relocation of both learned and popular art in the heart of mass culture.

In his book *Hybrid Cultures: Strategies for Getting In and Out of Modernity*, Nestor García Canclini suggests that hybridisation is not only the mixing of heterogeneous things but, more importantly, it is the improvement on or the falling into disuse of old encyclopaedias, old repertoires, and old classifications. Hybridisation implies that borders have been shifted. The hybrids that we are talking about are those that come about solely because of the destruction, or at least the erosion, of old identities. However, the stubborn conservative mentality persists in trying to reduce all types of combinations to new forms of the old. To understand these new mixtures, these new crosses, today's hybrids, we have to understand that it is all happening on the periphery. By contrast, the centre is still dreaming of its roots, still protecting itself, while the margins and frontiers are in the process of fusion and transformation. The industrialisation of culture through electronic communication has underlined more clearly the semantic and communicative dimension of living. As well as integrating a large contingency of populations, the mass communication networks of the cities put these people in touch with macro-urban experience.

Canclini suggests that having included arts and crafts in mass processes of message-circulation, their nutritive source of forms and images, their channels of diffusion and their audiences began to coincide. Also, art is produced within a zone networked with lines of dependence that link it to the market, cultural industries and references that are the very same for crafts. The plurality of references with whidh artists, craftworkers and mass media build their work obliges us to take a new look at the equivalent processes of disconnection and interlinking in contemporary societies. For Canclini, another important reason to study the art/craft situation as a socio-cultural problem and not only as an aesthetic question, is the necessity to take in a more extensive universe than that of singular products, consecrated as art. Many works with pretensions of being art are simply the repetition of anterior aesthetic models, with none of the attributes that justify the artistic label, but only the tedmique or the commercial process. In the same way, the majority of craft productions have no aesthetic aspirations. Even so, we can affirm that what we call art is not only that whidh culminates in great works, but also the space where society carries out its symbolic production.

However, deterritorialisation entails denationalisation; that is, the appearance of cultures with no territorial memory. In audiovisual cultures, for example, we note that different generations have made use of rock music with all its cultural trimmings and aesthetic derivations, its hybridisation with different local musical traditions and its use as a generation's banner. Faced with the belief and perception that there is no culture without territory, today we live through cultural experiences that are totally disconnected from territory. It is a process in which the old stereotypes tend to confuse no-national with anti-national, when in reality it is a new cultural experience. Today, how can we separate the destruction of old forms of identity from the appearance of new forms within the process of cultural industry? Certainly, there is destruction and homogenisation of identities in the process, but there are also new perceptions, new experiences, and new ways of acknowledging and recognising oneself. Despite all the manipulation, cultural orientations are taken on as a response to a certain moment in history and, at the same time, because of the process of internal evolution in art as a specialised activity. The market and its circuits are more active in discovering, adapting and hyperbolically promoting natural tendencies than artifically imposing them, although this latter activity may represent a considerably high percentage of mass cultural industry.

Crowning the Summit

When artists searched out forms and types of popular and mass culture, opening new critical frontiers to the dominant cultural discourse in political and cultural positions, they were seeking cultural expressions that were an alternative to institutional modernism. If postmodernism takes back on board and re-evaluates that which it has excluded up to now, it is true that it does so from an *avant-garde* experience of shaking off the dogma of popular culture as something regressive and alienating. Postmodern plastics would not have existed without the freedom, gained by the *avant-gardes*, to make art with just about anything. So postmodernism simply extends this supposed liberty of creation in a direction that modernism had opposed and, consequently, blocked off.

Artists who use ways, forms and practices from popular culture, do so fundamentally because of their symbolic connotations, and for the memory they carry, for the space to which they allude and for their effect on the public space. Ultimately they are attracted to the semantic content that their use involves and to their communicative efficiency. Every object is a reminder of its past; objects express an internal coherence created by their technique, their form, their different uses, their history, and the elements of memory they contain. No object or action has a closed meaning. Significance is not permanent; it can be pushed to its communicative limit when put into circulation with other objects. In changing contexts, an artefact can be the vehicle of an allegory. A tension on the surface, in the material physicality of the signifier, can produce some effect of meaning.

These artistic practices use textiles as a cultural vehicle. The semantic potential comes from the presence and memory of textiles in other social contexts. Textiles can allude to domestic and workplace decoration, rural professions, fashion, the human body, desire, gender and sexual representation, different social rites, ethnic representation and so on. Various representational and technically hybrid processes are being used, depending on the artist's operative strategies. These works are not aiming at demonstrating the physicality of textiles but using them to explore their historical connotations, their links with time, people and memory. These works respond to a process of hybridisation, appropriation, re-signification, neologism and inventions. This entails enriching the language of textiles along with the resulting enrichment of perception and knowledge of the world. What is being put forward is a

Faith Ringgold
The French Collection, Part 1, no. 7 (1991) (detail)
quilt

reflective collaboration with the spectator in which the artistic object gives up its status of an unequivocal message sent out unidirectionally, to present itself as part of the collective discussion or project. Its purpose is to open up opportunities for debate, not to supply the solutions.

Faith Ringgold, USA (an Afro-American artist). She constructs quilts made from old remnants, following the typical rural North American tradition. However, she does not carry out the usual geometric patterns but makes realist, narrative and hugely critical scenes about the history of art having been written and controlled by white males. For example, in 'The French Collection 1.7' Picasso appears painting his work 'Les Demoiselles d'Avignon' along with African masks. Her work is a play of mirror images: a black artist using a technique that has been classified by the dominant critical discourse as craft, and representing one of modern art's most paradigmatic artists painting one of his most important pieces. This painting, inspired by African craft and corporality, was considered in learned circles to be his 'masterpiece'.

Consuelo Jimenez Underwood, USA (Mexican father of Huichol origin, mother second-generation Chicano). The border, ever-present in her work, represents a hybrid of cultural space and the relentless divide between abundance and poverty, a line crossed daily by hundreds of people seeking to improve their living conditions. In her series 'Banderas de la Frontera' (Flags on the Border), she constructs a flag with both the Mexican and the North American flags. A barbed wire creates a transparent veil superimposed on the flag. She prints different images on the surface, emblematic symbols of Mexican and North American popular culture, which also belong to the Chicano culture, and dates that refer to specific moments in the history of the border between the two countries.

'Names Project Quilt', 1987, Washington D.C., formerly in Central Park, New York, 1994, and also Tokyo – the project is travelling round the world. Ten thousand rectangles of quilted cloth (3¢ x 7¢) sewn together to form a huge quilt, a great 'collage'. This gigantic community project commemorates about 20% of the people who have died from AIDS all over the world. At the beginning of the 1990s it was large enough to cover 10 football pitches. Each participant adds to the giant quilt a rectangle, for a relative or friend, or for someone famous.

Rosemarie Trockel, Germany. In the latter part of the 1980s her work began to centre on knitted paintings. She knits logos taken from the commercial and political world – the swastika, the hammer and sickle, the Playboy Bunny, Woolmark – multiplying them to decorate the surface of a painting. The confrontation of the feminine knit and the symbols of masculine politics and commerce is an ironic look at the construction of women's and men's social roles. The choice of medium – knitting – is also an ironical message about the primacy of painting as an important form of art and, in particular, about the virile connotations that art critics found in the abstract paintings of the 1950s and 1960s.

Paola Moreno, Chilean. In 'Atadura atávica' (Fancy fastenings) she reproduces pre-Colombian materials using contemporary textile language. She places tied-up piles of cloth on new cement stands where it is impossible to distinguish which are pre-Colombian designs and which are not. She shows formal connections between these textiles and the modern Bauhaus textiles. For the artist, the reconsideration of old South American textile art is an important project within contemporary American cultural education.

Observing the View (fragmented)

Postmodernity has introduced a more heterogeneous diversification in the centre-periphery and hegemony- subaltern relationships. But it has done so from the centre, reproducing its authority and hierarchy.

Beyond our preoccupation with the territorial limits of art, we could ask ourselves if the artistic function manages to modify its social standing, or just demystifies its commercial and ideological functions for the specialised public. To renounce the work of art as a ready-made product, the 'real truth' that the artist imposes on others, is a clear step forward. But what about the opening up of communication, the suggestion of new models of experience and reflection that generate other connections between art and society?

The present reorganisation of culture is not linear. The necessity for expanding cultural markets makes elitist goods more popular and introduces popular messages and products onto the cultivated scene. However, the struggle to control the cultivated and the popular is still being played through the definition and defence of specific symbolic capital and through underlining the differences which form the foundations of hierarchial positions. Even though the market must re-invent hierarchies to renew distinctions between groups, it has become more implausible to maintain that certain forms of narration, symbolising or reasoning are superior.

We cannot simply think of globalisation as a trans-territorial sphere with contacts in all directions. That does not happen. Globalisation does not consist of effective interconnection of all points through a netted web of communication and exchange. Rather, globalisation is a radical system that connects hegemonic centres to multiple, highly diversified zones. To transform the ideological structures that hold together old stereotypes, we must question the value of that which hegemonic culture excluded or underestimated. We must ask if hegemonic culture is capable only of reproducing itself or if it can also create the conditions necessary for unorthodox and marginal forms of art and culture to communicate and exhibit.

Walter Benjamin writes: 'Roofs, lightning conductors, railings, weather vanes, carvings: all ornaments are useful for scaling façades.´

OBLIVION AND METAMORPHOSIS: AUSTRALIAN WEAVERS IN RELATION TO ANCIENT ARTEFACTS FROM CYPRUS

Diana Wood Conroy

The importance of place, of families passing down knowledge was emphasised by a visit to the village of Fiti with its crowded kafeneion in the main square. Efterpi Christodoulou, the weaver, greeted us in delighted recognition, her loom in the corner of the cafe warm with a kerosene stove, men playing backgammon, a blue robed priest.

I was moved to see how Efterpi wove on the old loom exactly the way I do on mine, the rhythmic bang of the beater, the boat shuttles flying through the open space between the two sets of warp threads. Archaic movements. In ancient Greece the warp, so stretched and taut was masculine, while the soft and accommodating weft thread that passes through it was feminine. Both together made up the fabric of the state, according to Plato. Sexy weaving, the sign of matrimony and household order. Efterpi's mother taught her, she taught her daughters.
Excerpt from unpublished journal from Paphos expedition 1997,
Diana Wood Conroy

Craft traditions and skills passed on from mother to daughter, from father to son, from hand to hand, in 'immemorial usage, having almost the force of law' (one definition of 'tradition' in 1591), are remote from the mainstream of Australian non-Aboriginal contemporary practice. Modernity, and much postmodernity, can be defined by the rupture of this genealogical sequence, a loss of harmony, a lack of wholeness, a fragmentation. As Adorno wrote, the medium of tradition is not consciousness but the 'given unselfconscious obligatoriness of social forms'. Such social forms were traditional relationships and obligations embedded in craft skills, forming a mesh of associations within the community quite apart from the monetary value of crafts, and these relationships and obligations are no longer seen as significant in large-scale capitalist societies. 'Art has lost the traditionally guaranteed, self-evident truth of its relation to the object, to the material, and that of its methods, and must reflect them in itself![1] The emphasis on the present materiality of an artwork which refers to itself first as the 'original' work of a particular individual does not need even a nod to the past. The idea of innovation in 'modern' art is inscribed with not only the loss, but also the irrelevance of past traditions.

The rigorous refusal of tradition in contemporary art is expressed in the rejection of artforms that encompass tradition through their very construction, such as tapestry and textiles, which in Australia have often been relegated to a position away from mainstream *avant-garde* practice. The use of traditional media which require great skill may become a transgression that cannot be tolerated within the contemporary agenda. 'The relation to tradition is converted into a canon of the forbidden'.[2]

The first tiny ships bearing convicts and settlers to Australia, with masts like looms taut with sailcloth and rope warps tensed against the wind, made their way slowly south, at the end of the eighteenth century. As Ian McLean has pointed out, Australia had a repressed genealogy, and like Aphrodite in Cyprus, her European settlers emerged from the ocean, born of salt and foam. The Antipodes, the southern landmass that was assumed to exist by Greek geographers to balance the northern lands of Europe, were seen by English settlers as 'a sort of Cockaigne where traditional values upturned'. Customs of class and rank were inverted in this 'Antipodes', a land of thieves where convicts condemned in England could grow rich and free, and where it was noted that these convicts stunted by ill-treatment had children that grew tall and slender.[3]

Mute testimony of the everyday cloth of empire is found in a collection of fabric scraps from Hyde Park Barracks in Sydney, which served as housing for 'emigrant, indigent and infirm' women between 1848 and 1886. None of these fragments of cloth is handwoven, but many are handstitched. In a body of artwork that meditated on the materiality and process of these textile fragments, Anne Brennan bridged the gap between her mother's antecedents in Jewish communities in Russia and displaced women in colonial Australia. 'Secure the Shadow' was shown in 1995 at the Hyde Park Barracks.[4] Such an interaction between the past and present with its sometimes painful investigation into the half-forgotten traumas of family migration demonstrates the need to find a sign, an object from the past that will reverberate in the present and open up other countries of origin in a kind of archaeology of the layers of ancestry and self.

Many migrants, if not convicts, may have been dispossessed weavers. Paul Carter has connected the invention of the spinning machine or mule by Samuel Crompton in the 1770s to a sequence of events that eventually displaced cottage industry weavers and drove them to the towns, to the workhouse, and eventually to migration. 'Weaving is not simply a strand in colonial history, the pattern of Australia's European occupation may be woven on its loom... The mechanisation of spinning and weaving precipitated an internal colonisation but for which the sailcloth of empire might never have been raised'.[5] Nevertheless, colonial Australia had few workshop traditions of textiles, or industrial production, as imports from India and Manchester had always provided cloth since the end of the eighteenth century. Sewing and embroidery, though not weaving, were part of the domestic duties and expectations of women.

Maurice Blanchot has made the point that out of the forgetting – out of the oblivion of dislocation or war which is the starting point of so many journeys to Australia – may come a transformation, a metamorphosis. The diaspora of post-war Europe, too, resulted in a flow of emigrants to Australia. The 'forgetting' of so many traditions may have been necessary to hold against the terrible weight of the past, or even the awful clarity of having everything remembered, categorised, known, set down. 'Forgetting allows mortals to rest in the hidden part of themselves'.

Woven rug: Solvig Baas Becking

The arrival in the 1950s of professionally trained weavers laid the basis for an understanding and appreciation of weaving as a significant artform in Australia. The enthusiastic commitment for the craft of weaving in Australia from these women was the result of displacement and destruction, and of their migration to Australia. Living in a new country did not permit even the speaking of the mother tongues. 'Our world goes to pieces; we have to rebuild our world... the new comes about through exuberance and not through a defined deficiency,' wrote Anni Albers in 1944, after moving from Germany to the United States. Albers' belief in materiality and process, despite such extreme re-location, is evident: 'We often look for the underlying meaning of things while the thing itself is the meaning'.[7] Solvig Baas Becking, who had the same Bauhaus ethic as Albers, observed: 'The difficult problems are the fundamental problems – simplicity stands at the end, not at the beginning of a work... Each design element must serve a definite purpose in the whole concept...' ('Weaving', *Craft Australia* 1977/1)

Solvig Baas Becking (born 1928), whose origins are in Holland and Norway, was trained as a production weaver at Ekeby on the Norwegian border. She knew every part of the loom and was trained to think in terms of structure – twill, satin and plain weave being the three basic components of all weaves.

The rug is still the central form of her work, constructed with a labyrinthine combination of shaft switching and compensated inlay, so that the rich colour and image effects attained could be considered parallel to tapestry.

The bounded pattern in Solvig Baas Becking's rugs is based on a woven grid, which is overlaid by delicate or brilliant colour that adjusts the vertical warp patterns with another horizontal pattern element, resulting in a shift, an instability, even in meandering curves and spirals with an optical effect. Traditional weaving structures such as the undulating twill so prevalent in Baas Becking's rugs, have a thought-provoking longevity, going back seven thousand years in the Mesopotamian region.[8] In a wool rug woven in the early 1980s Baas Becking offered a reflection of this mix of technologies and cultures by juxtaposing a miniature traditional Turkish pile rug against a tapestry woven parquet floor. The knotted 'oriental' rug was then sewn on to the flat woven diamond panels representing the floor. The rug has absorbed and 'grounded' a range of techniques and traditions within the new vitality of an Australian context.

Techniques which actually construct the textile, such as tapestry, rug and fabric weaving, require a sense of order and pattern particular to textiles. Although the weaver has been displaced from her country of origin the woven structure itself is intrinsically a model for connection, for re-weaving after catastrophe a mesh of interconnecting threads. The grid of the weaving draft transcends language differences. Perhaps the old conjunctions of war and craft, of breaking down and building up can be faintly discerned here. Solvig Baas Becking left post-war Europe and established the complex skills of traditional European weaving construction in the Antipodean land.

Woven Tapestry: Kay Lawrence

Even in times of peace, journeys are part of the Australian psyche. Kay Lawrence (born 1947) is a tapestry weaver who has maintained a clear adherence to traditions passed down through Gobelin workshops of nineteenth-century France, to Edinburgh in Scotland, and from there to Australia. In 1977–78 Lawrence studied tapestry weaving with Maureen Hodge at the Edinburgh College of Art, Scotland, where tapestry traditions had been reinvigorated by Archie Brennan to absorb even 'pop' art and photography.

Journeys were part of her family background. Born in Canberra, Kay Lawrence left the capital when she was still a young child to live in New Guinea, and later in Malaysia, before returning to Australia and training at the South Australian School of Art. Her paternal grandfather was a Welsh miner and a hospital orderly in World War 1, and as his lungs had become bronchial he

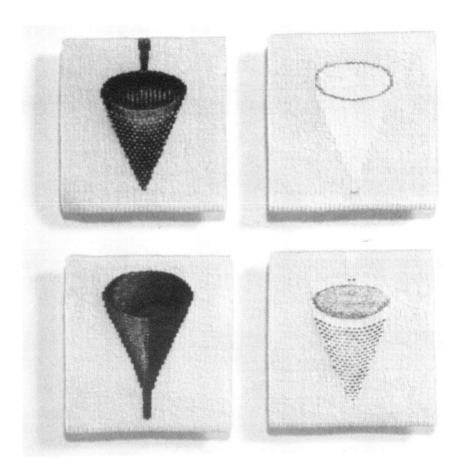

Kay Lawrence
Spill (1998) (detail)
woven tapestry, linen, cotton, wool
each square 18 x 18cm

was advised to move to a hot dry climate. In a radical but beneficial shift to Australia he became a railway ganger at the remote outpost of Oodnadatta and was joined by his wife and two small children from Yorkshire.

This family connection to the desert is embedded in Kay Lawrence's imagery of sparse, high-toned inland landscapes. In a series of memorable works since 1978 Kay Lawrence's tapestry has moved through a graphic outwardness in exploring images of national identity and landscape, as in her tapestry in the Prime Minister's apartments in Parliament House (1986) or her design in 1988 for the monumental embroidery also in Parliament House, Canberra, to private realms of subjectivity.

Her mother died when Kay was a young adult, and much of her work in the l990s turned on the exploration of the mother/daughter relationship, and the attempt to discover what is 'handed on' and what is irrevocably lost. The loss of the mother has become an underlying but forceful theme in Lawrence's tapestries.[9]

In 1998 Kay Lawrence wove a series of twenty-one small tapestries of funnel-shaped sieves, entitled 'Spill'.[10] The sieve, a container pierced by holes, is fundamental to food preparation, and a basic necessity in the kitchen. Ceramic vessels with holes to strain food, oil and wine are common in an archaeological context. Such objects of everyday life are imbued with allegories. Yves Abrioux has observed in relation to past traditions that 'Allegory... suggests formal avenues whereby art and poetry can come to terms with the loss of wholeness which lies at the very heart of the modern artist's enterprise'.[11]

The richness of the metaphor of the sieve and its association with women in European tradition was explored by Marina Warner.[12] The sieve was a symbol of chastity in the Roman legend of the Vestal Virgin, Tuccia, who was accused of adultery. She demonstrated her innocence, the wholeness of her maidenhead, by filling a sieve with water and carrying it without spilling. The sieve also demonstrated the ability to prudently sift good from evil. On the other hand, in Socrates' account, a vessel or pot full of holes is like 'the part of the soul in which our appetites reside', appetites which cannot be contained. The effluvia of the body may leak out, and be wasted, leading to emptiness and barrenness. Foolishness, in the limerick, is to go to sea in a sieve. A Greek myth has Hippotes curse his crew with 'leaky boats and rule by women'. The Danaids who killed their husbands on the first night of marriage to preserve their chastity were condemned forever in Hades to pour water from leaking pitchers into sieves.[13] The ambivalence of the sieve in these examples highlights Lawrence's use of it in 'Spill'.

The whole 'vessel' of the human body/psyche as an integrated entity, so exposed by psychiatry, has become fragmented, pierced with holes, in the images of contemporary art. Even the idea of maternity is perforated with doubt and 'does not hold water'. 'Vessels that leak,' wrote Kay Lawrence, 'like the sieve, can play on our anxieties about the dissolution of identity and suggest the impossiblity of maintaining a permanently fixed and stable sense of self'.[14]

The twenty-one tapestries of sieves are varied in tones of pale to black, iconic in the centre of each square, some with water. The fact that these sieves do not leak, that the pierced vessels miraculously hold water, may indicate that strategems are required in order to retain the wholeness of the self, to be open and yet not lose the vital liquid. In the old story of the virgins demonstrating their virtue, the clever ones first dipped their sieves in oil or wax, working with an astute knowledge of materials central to craft. 'Craft', after all, also has the meaning of craftiness, guile, cunning, and even duplicity.

In visual terms 'Spill' indicates a full spectrum of these sieve stories. The repetition-with-variation of the same image, against a flat background, seems to mimic the idea of an archaeological series, an array of domestic vessel shapes. The materiality of the close-packed tapestry weave with its Gobelin and Scottish antecedents, is emphasised. Such an everyday object as a sieve opens up what Michel de Certeau called 'local legends' in relation to the contructed order of social and spatial living. 'The surface of this order is everywhere punched and torn open by ellipses, drifts and leaks of meaning: it is a sieve-order'.[15]

The restitution that Kay Lawrence seeks through her use of tradition is a personal one. But like Solvig Baas Becking, she has walked through the 'deserted places of memory' to re-discover and re-create traditions, and in doing so, she gives form to a particular longing for a metaphorical past.

The Woven Eel Trap: Yvonne Koolmatrie

Those who keep traditions also guard memory. The anguish of many indigenous Australians is that the intricate knowledge of place and language has been forgotten. The knowledge has not been handed on, often intentionally by elders seeing the world they had once known utterly obliterated. 'When I die, all the stories will be gone, all lost and scattered,' I was told in 1978 at the Aboriginal community at Port Macleay in South Australia. This overwhelming loss of language and land, and the driving anger of it, is a hidden momentum in the strong revival of artforms, particularly basket weaving among these same Ngarrindjeri people.[16] Tradition here is a complex amalgam of relationships, techniques, customs and especially stories; oral, rather than written narratives.

Three Aboriginal women represented Australia at the Venice Biennale in 1997: Emily Kngwarreye from Central Australia, Judy Watson from northern Australia, and Yvonne Koolmatrie from the Ngarrindjeri people in the south around the River Murray and Lake Alexandrina.[17] The visibility of such Aboriginal artists as a significant force in the Australian artworld has led to the recognition of indigenous traditions, with emphasis on process and ritual, in the formation of 'cutting edge' contemporary arts practice. 'The most "traditional" kind of artist in Australia, an old woman living in a remote Aboriginal community, is now seen as the most revolutionary,' observed Terry Smith, speaking of Emily Kngwarreye.[18]

Yvonne Koolmatrie was born in 1944 at Wudinna on the Eyre Peninsula in South Australia. Her mother, Connie, was born at Rabbit Island, Meningie, and her father Joe Roberts was descended from the Pitjantjara people at Yalata and Andamooka. He was 'stolen' when he was eight and adopted by a white family.

In the traditional material culture of the Ngarrindjeri the weaving of river rushes for traps, as well as every kind of basket, including woven coffins and cloaks, was a vital task performed by both men and women, and documented in a film made in the 1930s of Clarence Long, a Ngarrindjeri elder of the Coorong area.[19] In 1981 Dorothy Kartinyeri, an older Ngarrindjeri woman, held a workshop because she felt it was essential that she pass on ancient learning concerning rush weaving to younger people before the knowledge disappeared. Yvonne Koolmatrie and Ellen Trevorrow, another important Ngarrindgeri weaver, both attended, and the technique of collecting, preparing and weaving the rushes became central to their lives.[20] The metre-long, traditional trumpet-shaped eel traps which were placed in the current of the river became transformed in Koolmatrie's work. Re-presented in a gallery context, the haunting form, once so functional, takes on other personal associations closely tied to land and kin, and the overcoming of loss and colonisation. Not least, for non-Aboriginal Australians, is the emergence of an almost forgotten traditional practice, that of coiled rush basketry, re-formed to be of major significance in a contemporary arts context.

Describing the loss of so many traditions Yvonne Koolmatrie said, 'So many of the stories have gone from Lake Alexandrina, even the secret stories. I still have some, from my mother, since it has been given to me to carry on the weaving'.[21] Her work has shown the significance for an individual artist of asserting strengths derived from the culture of the Ngarrindgeri. Despite the loss of land the community has survived and the process of finding and picking the rushes in cherished sites and weaving them in the company of other weavers and storytellers has a new, contemporary meaning in affirming identity. The eel trap is a sieve also – the water rushes through the spaces in the basketry, leaving the eel unable to escape. These artefacts, when hung in a gallery away from any flowing water, trap our expectations, bring us up short against the suspicion that it is the emptiness of this vessel that shapes its astonishing form. Not only are the infinite connections made in the binding of the rushes, like a metaphor for tying the unravelled culture together again, but the eel trap has trapped our slippery and ambivalent attitudes to traditional indigenous cultures and placed them in the forefront of our concerns about contemporary arts.

Oblivion: Classical Tradition

These three textile artist, Solvig Baas Becking, Kay Lawrence and Yvonne Koolmatrie, have given significance to objects enmeshed in domestic and local traditions – the twill rug, a tapestry sieve, a woven trap. Each of these forms is ancient, compelling in the present but equally grounded in the past, with antecedents that would have been recognisable to the weavers of classical European civilisation. Tradition is suddenly a fertile site, layered with almost forgotten but still resonant images, in the bringing to light of an oblique archaeology of self. Bart Cassiman described an exhibition of international artists in 1993 in just these terms: 'Contact with the art historical process is not for these artists a completed process but sometimes bewilderingly alive – it is as if there were no dividing line between the present and the past'.[22]

What might be the connection for Australian textile artists to an ancient Mediterranean past, a past in which textiles are so fragmentary? If the answer is to search for origins, feminist classicists might point out that the ancient glory of Western civilisation was also 'a formative moment in misogyny'.[23] The scholarly reconstruction of ancient art might well be clarified by considering other models for ancient societies, models derived from indigenous societies or feminist studies which examine the unconscious assumptions of Western European patriarchy. For myself, the obsessive interest of the Greco-Roman past is to re-imagine textiles not only as a pervasive metaphor used by ancient writers for interwoven social structures, but also as a primary means of representation. There is a yearning for traditions that can never be directly known, but only inferred from traces which are geographically remote from Australia. As if to compensate for the rupture of a connection with a European past and to strengthen our own sense of lineage, Australians have valued greatly the legacy of European classical civilisations, and have been active as classical scholars and archaeologists.

Almost like a pilgrimage, Australians return to the Mediterranean to rediscover and experience a sense of the past. 'Travel (like walking)', wrote Michel de Certeau, 'is a substitute for the legends that used to open up space to something different. What does travel ultimately produce if it is not, by a sort of reversal, "an exploration of the deserted places of my memory" – the return to nearby exoticism by way of a detour through distant places, and the "discovery" of relics and legends... What this walking exile produces is precisely the body of legends lacking in one own's vicinity...'[24]

The oblivion of deserted cities and artefacts is doubly poignant for textiles. In present-day Australia we are removed from ancient Europe in space and time, and also by the paucity of material culture from which we may gain imaginative and scholarly access to the textile traditions of the ancient world. What does remain – together with centrality of textiles imagery in classical mythologies – suggests a culture of textile production and usage which is deeply familiar and yet oblique and elusive. This tantalising view of an ancient textile culture holds particular meanings for contemporary artists.

The construction of the nineteenth-century antique past in Australia was formed in the Nicholson Museum at the University of Sydney, which had begun with the collections of Sir Charles Nicholson in the 1840s, and was one of the earliest museums in the southern hemisphere. Admittedly, textiles played a small role because of their essential transience in the archaeological record.

'Modern' art, as it emerged in Europe in the early twentieth century, associated the dominance of Greek and Roman traditions with a stifling academy of art which was permeated with classical literature and styles. In Australia, academic art, including a preference for classical styles known primarily through reproductions, enjoyed conservative prestige much longer. Indeed, they were seen as a bulwark against European modernism. Eventually, in Sydney by the 1960s, the reproductions of 'classical' art history also seemed an irrelevance. Nineteenth-century plaster casts of all the great antique sculptures which had lined the Nicholson Museum at the University of Sydney – the *Laocoon*, the *Dying Gaul*, the *Hermes* of Praxiteles, the Cnidian *Venus* – had been brought to Sydney to validate a civilised enterprise, to lift the convict spectre of the colony. In the burst of new growth and optimistic expansion in the 1960s the plaster statues were dispersed to high schools, where many were vandalised, and soon vanished. Some were even used as fill for a new road in the University. Parallel to the tradition-scorning excitement in the visual arts, a surge of activity in the crafts area resulted in wonderfully confident large-scale textiles – the so-called 'hairy monsters', the product of an anti-traditional, archivally unsound, exuberant moment.[25] In Mediterranean cultures, too, the relevance of traditional hand weaving has been undermined by the experience of modernity. I would argue that such eras of destruction enable us to look again at the past. The blank spaces of disregard and loss may galvanise a fresh consideration of less obvious Mediterranean traditions:

> The middle aged and elderly women of Fiti and Lefkara in Cyprus say how they love the craft of weaving and embroidery, of preserving the old patterns. The hands of the Fiti weaver never stop skimming over the warp and weft, inserting and collecting the shuttles. 'But

for my daughters the process is too slow, too difficult and tiring. When the old ones who are now so skilled at certain motifs die, those patterns will die too.' The technique of weaving or embroidery itself holds no gratification if social custom does not give rewards – status, ritual significance – for the arduousness of the labour. You can earn more money in the big new tourist hotels on the coast.

Such a fading of traditions is countered by the fact that in Australia European traditions such as tapestry weaving have been re-located and re-invented as sign and metaphor through the substantial contributions of artists of whom Kay Lawrence is a foremost example. The development of women artists such as the energetic professionalism of Solvig Baas Becking and other emigrant weavers who left war-damaged Europe has allowed a new awareness of the positioning and sign of textiles to emerge. For indigenous artists too, Yvonne Koolmatrie has demonstrated how traditional techniques become systems of meaning in themselves, as the embodiment of genealogical narratives and a new apprehension of the possibilities of re-interpreting the past to hold off the traumas of the present.

The imaginative and creative nature of memory involves not only remembering but also forgetfulness and loss. In Cyprus, the artefacts are placed in museums, the meaningless looms are cast out to rot, the daughters no longer learn, a tradition stops. But in Australia a glimpse of ancient textiles sets off a new train of thought in the late twentieth century. Fragmentary artefacts of spindle whorls and loom weights evoke a shimmer, an echo, a reflection of what has been forgotten and may be reremembered.

Spindles, Whorls, Loom Weight and Linen Fragment: Unearthing the Forgotten

The travel by Australians, myself included, across oceans and continents to Cyprus to excavate a Greek theatre is in itself a reversal of the nineteenth-century movement to colonise and civilise the distant Antipodes.

Archaeologists aim to recover the material evidence of past cultures as a way of comprehending distant times and spaces. Classical archaeology in Europe unearths artefacts emblematic of cultures in which an oral tradition of 'handing down' existed beside a sophisticated literacy. To investigate the roots – or perhaps the spreading rhizomes – of traditional practices and our assumptions about them, I have sought insight into textiles production and use through a study of artefacts from a continuing Australian archaeological excavation of a Greek theatre in Paphos, Cyprus.[26]

The discovery by Australian archaeologists at this site of small textile-re-
lated objects in carefully described deposits is another event in the theatre's
history. As a weaver and an archaeologist, I am deeply moved by the finding
of these objects. Drawing the objects is not only a means of recording them
but also a way of knowing them intimately. The processes of excavating the
site and recording its yield are another kind of intense performance in the
ancient theatre. And, just as the theatre enables us to see more deeply into
ourselves, so archaeology fosters a deep understanding of our present lives.
This is how I responded to these findings of spindles, whorls and loom
weight at the Paphos site.

All that was visible of this site in 1995 was a few rock-cut steps in the
side of a grassy hill with fragmentary Greek inscriptions indicating, by their
letter forms, a date towards the end of the fourth century BC. An excavation
into such a hardly discernible site is fitting as an investigation into hidden
traditions. The opacity and density of the earth requires a meticulous process
of digging, and this process is a discriminating craft in itself. The obscurity
of the structures and lack of certainty into what the site may hold is restful
and anticipatory at the same time.

Pottery fragments packing the striated layers of trenches are the primary
material of the site in making sense of patterns of trade and activity within
the theatre, which was in use from about 300 BC to 400 AD. Amongst the
large quantity of pottery, glass, bone, and marble fragments recovered from
the site are a group of objects associated with spinning and weaving. In
an unstratified deposit at a house area built after 400 AD at the top of the
seating, a loom weight was excavated. In the trenches near the site of an
ancient Roman road, spindle whorls and bone pins emerged together with
fragmentary Roman pottery and coins.

The six objects comprise three stone spindle whorls (two marble, one
soapstone), a bone pin or spindle, and an oval loom weight. The spindles
or shafts that were pushed through the hole of the whorls were no doubt
made of perishable wood. Dating spindle whorls is often difficult, despite
a profusion of examples, because the forms of spindle whorls and loom
weights hardly change over many centuries. Even when these objects are
found in datable contexts, it seems likely that they may have been handed
down in the family and be substantially older than the date suggests. Like
many other tools, once the form and function are well matched, the need
for change is slight, and if the technology of making cloth does not change,
nor do the tools of spinning and weaving.

From earliest times spindle whorls showed a diversity of material and
decoration, which was due to the fact that a spindle whorl was a personal

object which could be chosen according to fancy. According to Chavane the variations in form are not chronological, but exist at all periods and in many materials – faience, stone, terracotta and bone. Stone spindle whorls from Geometric to Byzantine from Salamis are nearly identical in form, and the shape continues in modern Greek wooden whorls. 'At the same time the art of spinning does not really evolve since its origins – the types, diverse in themselves are maintained for a thousand years, with all the forms and decorations being used in al1 these epochs', wrote Chavane after summing up the evidence from Salamis.[27]

Spindle whorls are used to weigh down the spinning rod, or spindle which forms the principal action of spinning fibre into thread. Most spindles would have been of wood and have not survived. Elizabeth Barber, in her comprehensive study of prehistoric textiles, has pointed out that the weight of the spindle whorl is all-important in giving a tension to the spinning thread and in judging what kind of thread may have been spun. Very fine threads of linen and silk need less weight than sturdy wool yarn. Weight is also the issue with loom weights which were used to give the warp threads tension for weaving on the vertical looms that existed until the first century AD.

The spinners of Paphos were spinning fine fibres from linen or cotton. In Salamis to the west it is also obvious that the needles, bone bobbins and small whorls from the Late Roman period must have been associated with a very fine thread, most likely linen, cotton or silk. Alexander the Great was known to have had a great weakness for silk. 'Alexander conquered the Medes and the Median dresses conquered Alexander,' reported the Roman Tertullian. Very expensive Chinese silk had made its way to the Greek world since the fourth century BC, and the transparent quality of silken women's garments was supposed to have shocked the people of Messene.[28] The comparatively coarse woollen thread spun on spindles in present-day Greek villages does not give an indication of the gossamer thinness of thread required in sophisticated clothing fabric. A truer modern comparison would be handspun cotton and silk fabrics from India.

It is known that loom weights were generally obsolete by the first century AD with the introduction of the horizontal loom.[29] But it may well be that the two types of loom co-existed for generations, so this loom weight has no definite date. Made by hand of a coarse heavy clay, in an ovoid form, the loom weight from the theatre site has a smooth, finely cut hole near one of the long faces. There are traces of a worn groove such as might have been made by a cord or thread tied through the hole, where the weight was hung to give tension to the warp threads.

The loom weight as an object is difficult to date, as different types exist together in the same site. The predominance of one type seems due more to local custom than to chronological evolution. 'One mustn't forget the solidity of these large objects – a set of weights were probably transferred from mother to daughter and a weight lost or damaged was easily replaced; this explains the lack of evolution of these objects'.[30] Loom weights are usually made by hand, from the same kind of coarse clay used to make *pithoi*, or storage vessels.

Archaeologists use these traces of material culture to form insight into ancient processes of production of thread and cloth. Though not from the Paphos theatre site, there is a rare fragment of material woven of linen found in a Roman house nearby that complements these finds because it offers a glimpse of the cloth worn on the body in everyday living.[31] The tiny scrap was found on the skeleton of a man who died when the wall collapsed on him during an earthquake. 'Clasping his hands above his head, he had sought protection of the wall but the tremor was too strong to spare him'.[32]

The cloth has been crushed into small folds, which are very clear when the piece is backlit. The linen thread has slight irregularities and a rigid quality familiar to me, as a weaver who has struggled to maintain an even tension in linen. The olive-green colour is still vivid, merging into a more turquoise hue, which may be due to fragments of copper to be seen under a magnifying glass. Such a dye colour could have been achieved through a combination of indigo with a yellow dye, possibly saffron. The colour may have been intensified through the action of the metallic compounds, which acted as a mordant, or fixer, to intensify the colour in the fibre. Copper and iron are both used as mordants for 'vegetable' or 'natural' dyes.

Together with twelve coins, three of silver and nine of bronze, fragments of linen cloth were found preserved as a result of being impregnated with copper oxide. The coins, dated from 31 BC to 38 AD, may have been in the pocket of the garment or perhaps in a linen bag. This piece of cloth provides invaluable evidence for an everyday fabric, a linen garment or bag preserved through chance rather than as carefully chosen grave goods or as a dedicatory offering to a deity.

To find the cloth so associated with the skeleton underlines the fundamental association of fabric with the body. The man with had coins in his pocket was involved in the exchange of goods, in the everyday desires of small purchases. It is the presence of coins, the evidence of his active participation in the commercial life of the time that has preserved the cloth, through their toxic emissions. More frequently, ordinary woven cloth becomes invisible, continually remade, re-cycled and broken down – it is the significant process of construction, as a metaphorical act, that lasts in the writings of the time. Plain weave cloth providing warmth, protection and status, is as basic as cooking – also associated with the flux of the body, and equally ephemeral in the material evidence of the past. The preserved fragments of cloth are like minute fragments of the unknown man's energy and longing, an emotion still so familiar to us as we finger coins in our own pockets. The interlocking of the plain weave structure is like the criss-crossing grid of streets where this man died. We can find very similar pieces of cloth in shops near us today – the common ground of unstyled ordinariness that we can still identify as persisting, unspoken, like a sign of unconsciousness.

The unchanging forms of spindles, whorls and loom weights appear to offer evidence that textile techniques do not develop, but this of course gives no indication of the relationships embedded in the craft processes, nor of changing materials and styles. Paphos was continually 'interrupted' by earthquakes, by changing political fortunes and trade allegiances. Three points can be made in comprehending the place of textiles in Greco-Roman Paphos.

First, the relationship of women to textiles in ancient Paphos does not necessarily reflect the demeaning character and domestic connotations of textiles in historical Western societies – the making of textiles may have been as fulfilling and satisfying or as difficult for women as public life was difficult and fulfilling for men. The overwhelming evidence suggests that one of the primary tasks of free women in the Greek and Roman world was to organise the making of cloth for household use. Ritual life was also of a dominating importance to women, and the votive dedications to deities, particularly Hera, Artemis and Athena, of woven cloth and implements of spinning and weaving, mitigated misfortune and the crises of life. Everyday life in this long period held many variations, both economic and social, and in hybrid Cyprus particularly, Phoenician influences lingered in the nearby towns of Larnaca and Amathus, and the customs and rites of the famous temple of Aphrodite may have allowed other versions of femininity to exist.

The secluded woman is an upperclass woman. By contrast many freed-women and slaves engaged in a great diversity of occupations which frequently took place in streets, market places and large houses. The colour of those narrow paved streets is brought to life by inscriptions from across the Greek and Roman world which indicate the variety of ways of making a living for ordinary women. Despite the stereotypical view of ancient women as confined to the spaces of the family home, many occupations have been identified from inscriptions which give a vivid picture of the specialisation of women's life, presumably in small stalls or shops on the streets. Examples of the diverse occupations of freedwomen, if not the wives of citizens, include sesame seed seller, grocer, horsetender, perfume vendor, musician, honey seller, frankincense seller, shoe seller, salt vendor, gilder of helmets, grocer, as well as concubine, procuress, wet nurse, harp and lyre player. Occupations directly relating to textiles included woolworker, seamstress, weaver, spinning girl, and garland weaver.[33] If we imagine the variety and life of the streets, the clear oppositions between public/private, male/female may begin to blur.

Secondly the production of textiles was as important in satisfying ritual needs as in the construction of complex feminine roles in the household economy. The significance of textiles in the material evidence of archaeology is doubly hidden. Not only are textiles hardly preserved from excavated sites, but also their significance may have been in the relationships formed by their making. Intricately woven textiles were dedicated to deities regularly, as we know from inscriptions and literature. Annette Wiener has described contemporary small-scale societies in which 'cloth possessions act as transcendent treasures, historical documents that authenticate and conform for the living the legacies and powers associated with a group or individual's connections to ancestors and gods'.[34] The reflections of such textiles in the ancient world may be glimpsed in painting, ceramics and especially in the mosaic tradition – textiles are the 'software' that has vanished, that once subtly programmed the surviving images in 'hard' materials of tesserae, ceramic and marble [see colour plate no. 8].

Given its significance in ritual and everyday life, it is not surprising that the idea of weaving should occupy a central place in Greek thought, as has been argued by John Schneid and Jesper Svenbro in a detailed analysis of both philosophical texts and mythology.[35] The skill of weaving was regarded by Plato as a metaphor for the fabric of the state itself, with the strong and vertical (male) threads of the warp supporting the more pliable and flexible (female) weft threads. One of Aristotle's favourite metaphors was 'the ship of state', and the mast of the ship, *histos*, is the same word as 'loom'. The Orphics regarded the warp thread tied to the loom weights as 'sperm'. The wider political fabric is composed of like and unlike groups of people woven together. The comedy of Aristophanes' *Lysistrata* had analysed the various parts of the carding, spinning and weaving of wool as a way of resolving bitter conflict. In all the struggles for political control in the Hellenistic and early Roman period, weaving could still be a 'sign' that demonstrated the bringing together of dissimilar elements – warp and weft – into a unified whole, of a kind of 'coitus' as the Roman philosopher Seneca observed.[36]

It could be said that Greek thought was itself like drapery, an expressive and flexible device particularly at the time when the Paphos theatre was founded in the Hellenistic age. Parallel to the sophistry and rhetoric of the orators and philosophers of this time, was a stylistic rhetoric in the visual arts which was achieved through an amplification and exaggeration of feature. Flowing, moving drapery animates the human form in sculpture, painting and mosaics of Greece and Rome, almost as if it had a life of its own. Known as 'wilful drapery' it forms a great curve around the head of a goddess or nymph, or accentuates the diagonal movement of a warrior with a flying cloak. Sculptural representations of drapery that cling to the body and extend its action indicate how fundamental cloth was to notions of identity and character. Marble carving, and even terracotta figurines, skilfully showed the layers of different cloth, the fine 'woven wind' of muslin, almost transparent, laid over the thick woollen undergarment, veiling yet revealing the face and breasts of a woman.

Lastly, the 'wholeness' of the Cypriot tradition was as open to influences and materials from Cilicia, Syria, Egypt and Rhodes, and further afield in Italy, western Europe and northern Africa as any hybrid community in the contemporary world. Indigenous cultures of Australia were regarded by many European observers as having unchanging and intact traditions, which were unable to be influenced by outside forces. Traditions of craft in the ancient Mediterranean may still be regarded fallaciously as 'pure, discrete and intact',[37] as so many 'third world' cultures have been positioned in the recent past, including Aboriginal cultures. We have no proof that 'tradition' was seamless and untroubled in ancient Cyprus.

Thinking about Ancient Tradition in an Australian Context

My aim in this essay has been to show that the investigation of ancient and obscured textile traditions, as in this study of the Paphos artefacts, can lead to a transformation of perceptions in the observer. Contemporary arts practice, exemplified by Solvig Baas Becking, Yvonne Koolmatrie and Kay Lawrence, shows how 'tradition' may be almost obliterated and forgotten and can then revive again in a metamorphosis of its original form.

Can we demonstrate by a comparison with contemporary weavers that 'classical' traditions may be composed of hybrid elements, interspersed with doubtful episodes, despite the continual 'handing on'? Does an examination of a particular textile tradition uphold the idea of an unchanging and constant passing of skills, or is the record ruptured, and skills passed on despite, or because of the continual fragility of societies in the face of war, conquest, pestilence and natural disaster?

The example of the craft revival in Australia post-war shows how, at a point when textile handcrafts in Australia seemed all but lost, a new fervour arose. Solvig Baas Becking's life in Australia, vigorously demonstrating and exhibiting the techniques of weaving learnt in 1940s Europe, contributed substantially to the great revival of craft in the 1960s and 70s. Although not so much an economic necessity as a metaphorical need for 'handcrafts', the traditions of spinning and weaving taught by refugees from war and dev-astation, emphasised and enhanced the peaceful society. The tools of craft – such as the spindle, the whorl, the loom weight – became metaphors for relationship and connection. We can see that in an ancient society haunted by earthquake and changing powers, tradition may be the groundswell of economic and social security.

In considering ancient Mediterranean textile traditions, the model of the interconnection between craft, myth and relationship (kinship and geneal-ogy) in indigenous communities may well be more cogent than an assump-tion of Western art history hierarchies. Bella Zweig, in a study which uses non-Western models to look at the position of women in ancient Greece, has pointed out that indigenous societies may provide a more appropriate means of perception for ancient Greek society than modern Western approaches. For example, in religion and ritual 'women may have enjoyed powers and esteem in ways unmatched by any comparable activity in the contemporary Western world'. In Australia we are only recently aware of the equality in ritual matters held by women in many Aboriginal societies, because of the fact that the observers of these societies were male anthropologists and explorers, who had little access to Aboriginal women and therefore did not 'see' them.[33] The same humanist scholarship that educated those colonial administrators and ethnographers in Australia has been responsible for forming our ideas of the ancient Mediterranean past.

The fragmented traditions of the Ngarrindjeri in South Australia have found a new voice in the contemporary pieces of Yvonne Koolmatrie, con-clusively denying the 'dying race' prophecies which had been so prevalent in ethnography and government.[39] An innovative vitality is achieved by re-positioning ancient forms of eel traps in present-day gallery and museum contexts. The resuscitation of an almost forgotten technique of rush basketry is seen by her as an affirmation of the mythologies and relationship to place which had nearly fallen into oblivion. The responsibility to family and clan, so unimportant in mainstream Western art, is central. From this example we can see that considering family, ritual and domestic responsibilities in ancient societies might result in a very different interpretation of evidence.[40]

The abeyance and the disregard of classical traditions in 'modern art' of the mid-twentieth century has allowed other aspects and forms of tradition to emerge. The astonishing re-emergence of tapestry in Australia since 1970 as a technique that is in a practical sense hardly any different to the technique used by Athena, Arachne or Penelope shows the traditional force or the 'aura' of the sign 'tapestry'. Although the tapestry technique in Europe has been associated with a powerful, conservative and decorative tradition, Kay Lawrence has demonstrated subtle nuances of image and structure that question safe assumptions. She has demonstrated the force of the medium as a sign of lament, as a way of warding off trauma very comparable to the ritual, apotropaic and funerary functions of textiles in the ancient world. The life of women in Greco-Roman times, so long invisible, is also re-emerging due to a reappraisal of classical studies. This examination of the evidence of past traditions may bring up unpredictable, even uncomfortable aspects which provide a friction, a kind of electrical charge to our own present. Despite long periods of forgetfulness and neglect of textile traditions we can begin tentatively to construct another understanding of the past. In contemporary tapestry, the notion of 'tradition' may become a transgressive and lively element in both content and form.

The neo-classical idea of antiquity brought to Australia in the nineteenth century is remote from a late twentieth-century view of this past, a view informed by familiarity with indigenous cultures and seen through feminised eyes. The metaphor of weaving still reverberates not only in the intricate material forms of thread and cloth, but also through digital webs and sites in the electronic field. The darkness of Australia, the terra nullus or land of no-one, a land without a human memory to its white invaders, is a site of oblivion which may just possibly allow metamorphoses, transformations from all the forgettings, all the loss, in a fresh sequence of 'handing on.'

> An Aboriginal friend was asking me about my work on Paphos. I said to her 'I don't know what the connection is between such different interests, between my absorption in Aboriginal issues, and the close involvement in Cyprus'. 'It's easy to see the connection,' she said. 'The connection is the ocean, the sea that touches the edge of the land in both places.'

Acknowledgements

With much appreciation to Dr Sophocles Hadjisavvas, Head, Department of Antiquities in Cyprus for permission to photograph and study objects from the Paphos

Museum. Particular thanks to Professor Richard Green, Director of the Paphos Theatre Expedition from the University of Sydney for encouraging overlaps between art and archaeology. I am very grateful to Kay Lawrence and Dorothy Jones for reading and commenting on the text, and to Sue Rowley for her astute editing.

Notes

1. Theodor W. Adorno, 'On Tradition' in *The Sublime Void: On the memory of the imagination*, (ed. Bart Cassiman), ex cat., Koninklijk Museum, Antwerp, Belgium. p. 74.
2. *Ibid.*, p. 75. The intricacies of this relationship to textile media are discussed in Diana Wood Conroy, 'Curating Textiles: Tradition as transgression', *Object*, no. 4, 1994–95, pp. 19–23.
3. Ian McLean, *White Aborigines: Identity Politics in Australian Art*, Cambridge University Press, Cambridge, New York and Melbourne, 1998, pp. 4–5.
4. Anne Brennan, 'Running stitch and running writing: thinking about process' (ed. Sue Rowley), Craft and Contemporary Theory, Allen and Unwin, 1997, pp. 93–97.
5. Paul Carter, 'The Promise of Fruit', ex. cat., *The Promise of Fruit*, North Adelaide School of Art Gallery, South Australia,13 May – 4 June 1998.
6. Maurice Blanchot, 'Oublieuse Memoire, l'entretien infini, Paris', *The Sublime Void: On the memory of the imagination* (ed. Bart Cassiman), ex. cat., Koninklijk Museum, Antwerp, 1993, p. 87.
7. Anni Albers, *On Designing*, Wesleyan University Press, Connecticut, 1961, p. 30.
8. E.J.W. Barber, *Prehistoric Textiles: The development of cloth in the Neolithic and Bronze ages, with special reference to the Aegean*, Princeton University Press, New Jersey, U.S.A.1990, p. 383.
9. These tapestries have been documented in Sue Rowley, *Crossing Borders: Contemporary Australian Textile Art*, ex. cat., University of Wollongong, Wollongong, 1995; Diana Wood Conroy, 'Kay Lawrence', *Identities: Artfrom Australia* (ed. Deborah Hart), Taipei Fine Arts Museum, Taipei, 1993; Diana Wood Conroy, 'Texts from the Edge: contemporary Australian tapestries', ex. cat., Jam Factory Adelaide 1994; Anne Brennan, 'Embodying and Spilling', *Kay Lawrence*, ex. cat., Canberra School of Art Gallery, Canberra, 1998.
10. Woven when Lawrence was the HC Coombs Creative Fellow at the Australian National University in 1998
11. Yves Abrioux, *Ian Hamilton Finlay: A visual primer*, The MIT Press, Cambridge, Mass. 1992, p. 293.
12. Marina Warner, *Monuments and Maidens*, Weidenfeld and Nicolson, London, 1985, pp. 242–244.
13. Plato, Gorgias (transl. and intro. Walter Hamilton), Penguin, 1971, pp. 92–3, cited in Marina Warner, ibid., p. 249.
14. 'Spill' was exhibited at the Canberra School of Art Gallery in 1998 on the occasion of Kay Lawrence's residency as the Nugget Coombs Research Fellow at the Australian National University, 1998.
15. Michel de Certeau, *The Practice of Everyday Life* (transl. Stephen Rendall), University of California Press, Berkeley 1988, p. 107.
16. Diana Wood Conroy with Ellen and Tom Trevorrow, 'Both Ways; Yolngu and Ngarrindgeri', *Craft and Contemporary Theory, op. cit.*, pp. 155–170.
17. Hetti Perkins, (ed.), *Fluent, La Biennale di Venezia 1997, Australia*, ex cat., Art Gallery of New South Wales, Sydney, 1997.
18. Terry Smith and Margo Neale 1998, ABC radio interview, Australia, 21 February 1998.
19. This film is held in the archives of the South Australian Museum, Adelaide.

20. Diana Wood Conroy with Ellen and Tom Trevorrow, 'Both ways: two cultures: Yolngu and Ngarrindjeri weaving in Australian arts practice', *op. cit.*

21. Conversation with Yvonne Koolmatrie at conference 'Weaving culture' at Camp Coorong, South Australia, Dec. 1997.

22. Bart Cassiman (ed.), 'Introduction', *The Sublime Void: on the memory of the imagination*, ex. cat, Koninklijk Museum, Antwerp, 1993, p. 5.

23. Nancy Sorkin Rabinowitz and Amy Richlin (eds), *Feminist Theory and the Classics*, Routledge, New York, 1993, p. 9.

24. Michel de Certeau, *The Practice of Everyday Life* (transl. Stephen Rendall), University of California Press, Berkeley, 1988, pp. 106–7.

25. At the same time a rigorous tradition from Scotland and France of tapestry woven in workshops, strongly related to modernist painting, was introduced in the 1970s, particularly through the Victorian Tapestry Workshop.

26. The Paphos Theatre Expedition in Cyprus is directed by Professor Richard Green of the University of Sydney and supported by the Australian Research Council 1995–2001.

27. Marie-Jose Chavane, 'Les Petits Objets', *Salamine de Chypre*, vol. vi. Diffusion de Boccard, Paris, 1975, p. 88.

28. Gullberg, E. and Astrom, P., 'The thread of Ariadne: a study in ancient Greek dress', *Studies in Mediterranean Archaeology*, XXI, Goteborg, Sweden, 1970, p. 17.

29. Gladys R. Davidson, 'The Minor Objects', *Corinth*, vol xii, American School of Classical Studies at Athens, Priceton, New Jersey, 1952, p. 146.

30. Marie-Jose Chavane, *op. cit.*, p. 78.

31. K. Nicolaou, 'Excavations at Nea Paphos: The House of Dionysos, Outline of the campaigns 1964–65', *Report of the Department of Antiquities in Cyprus*, Department of Antiquities, Nicosia, Cyprus, 1967, pp. 100–125. These objects come from the celebrated House of Dionysos, not far from the theatre site, where extensive mosaics, including a procession of Dionysos, indicated a substantial Roman palace built in the mid-second century over previous dwellings on the same site. Those who lived in these houses must often have formed the audience of the theatre, connected through a grid of paved streets. The context of the ancient city and the ruins of particular buildings form an intriguing background to the artefacts. The vivid life of the present town of Paphos intersects with the ancient sites, forming another layer in the echoes of the same Greek language and through persistent village memories.

32. *Ibid.*, p. 108.

33. R. Lefkowitz and M. B. Fant, *Women's Life in Greece and Rome*, Duckworth, Great Britain, 1992, pp. 221–224.

34. A. Weiner, *Inalienable Possessions: the paradox of keeping while giving*, University of California Press, Berkeley, 1992, p. 3.

35. John Schneid and Jesper Svenbro, *The Craft of Zeus: Myths of weaving and fabric*, Harvard University Press, Cambridge, Mass. 1996. (A detailed analysis of both philosophical texts and mythology.)

36. *Ibid.*, p. 13.

37. Pennina Bartlet, 'Rugs R Us (and them): the Oriental carpet as sign and text', *Third Text*, vol. 30, 1995, p.14.

38. Diane Bell, *Daughters of the Dreaming*, Mc Phee Gribble/George Allen and Unwin, Melbourne, 1993, pp. 229–255.

39. A.P. Elkin, *The Australian Aborigines: how to understand them*, Angus and Robertson, Sydney (1943) 1961, pp. 321–338. A survey of the policies since white settlement is given by Elkin, one of the architects of government policy towards Aborigines.

40. Bella Zweig, 'The Primal Mind: using native American Models for the study of women in ancient Greece', *Feminist Theory and the Classics* (ed. Nancy Sorkin Rabinowitz and Amy Richlin), Routledge, New York, 1993, pp. 145–181.

A QUESTION OF ABSENCE – OR, WHY IS THERE NO TEXTILE IN HONG KONG?

Hazel Clark

Introduction

In August 1994 an exhibition called *Fibre Art: Transforming Nature's Gifts* was held in Hong Kong.[1] It featured the work of seven female textile artists from Britain, and one from Poland, but significantly no one local or Chinese. As Anne Harte, a British textile artist resident in Hong Kong, commented, 'It is rare to see contemporary textiles on show in Hong Kong'.[2] This was true, for textile art does not seem to have a place in the territory, either in exhibitions or as creative practice. Since the show, the question has nagged – but why not? What are the conditions which generate and support contemporary textile art? Are they in any way 'foreign' to Asia, particularly to the newly developing economies? This essay aims to search out some answers.

The theoretical context is provided by the political discourse of Hong Kong. Colonial and postcolonial theory is relevant, but only up to a point. For Hong Kong is in a unique political situation of having relinquished Western imperialism to be handed over to a new colonial power, called 'its mother country'.[3] The work of local writers and critics provide another, in many ways more useful, framework for understanding how art, craft and other forms of cultural production intertwine with the political and economic context, and affect each other. The Joint Declaration and the Basic Law both provided that the government of the Hong Kong Special Administrative Region (SAR) should formulate culture policies, but do so 'on it own', without interference for the Central Government of China.[4] But autonomy is a difficult concept for a place which questions its own identity.

As local writer Ackbar Abbas has noted, Hong Kong is in a unique situation, as a former colony, but with no precolonial past to speak of.[5] It has previously been described as 'on borrowed time, in a borrowed place',[6] made up of sojourners, a 'cultural desert' with little political will and no sense of permanence. Abbas comments on how colonialism engendered an 'import mentality'. In other words, anything which came from outside was afforded greater respect than that which was generated in the colony. Although Hong Kong can be considered a global city and a premier financial hub in South East Asia, many areas of life have not developed apace with business and commerce. It was not until as late as the 1970s, for instance, that Hong Kong began to gain the confidence to generate its own culture.[7] Today, Hong Kong's cultural production is in a generative state as more younger resident artists and members of the diaspora search for ways to represent themselves. Certain artistic conventions and traditions are well established, but others, such as textile art, are not in evidence.

Art/Craft Debate

In the West, textile art has gained recognition as a distant branch of the 'fine' crafts. In Asia, this is not the case. Textile practice remains vested almost exclusively in either traditional textile crafts, or in industrial production. This is largely the result of market forces, such as tourism and the dictates of Western markets. Notable exceptions are Japan and Korea, where textile art and traditional textile crafts co-exist and are equally valued. Other countries, such as Indonesia, Thailand and Malaysia, which continue their strong textile traditions, have not witnessed the development of textile art. While Hong Kong is not a typical in Asia, consideration of its absence of textile art raises issues which have a resonance elsewhere.

Art and craft, regardless of their distinctions and similarities, are forms of cultural production. The appearance of the works produced are dependent on materials, skill, technique, content, creator, but also on the place of origination. The issues of place and cultural context are fundamental to the absence of textile art. In many South East Asian countries there is an apparent paradox within existing textile practice. One is the continuing strength of traditional textile crafts which still function at a high level and are very sophisticated, not simply 'folk art'. But the same countries, notably Indonesia, Malaysia and the Philippines, are rapidly developing economies whichdepend on the massproduction of cheap export fabrics. Here textile practice separates into traditional crafts produced in the rural setting versus cheap fabric mass-produced in the urban environment. The fine arts also tend to be circum-scribed either within indigenous tradition or by Western visual language.

These three 'movements' – traditional craft textiles, commercial production and the contemporary visual arts – tend to operate in isolation from one an-other. Ironically, they appear to have no points of commonality because there is no shared cultural space. What is absent is what Homi Bhabha has called the 'Third Space', the 'inter', or the 'cutting edge of translation and negotiation', that space wherein the colonised group can find its own voice.[8]

Craft Tradition in China

The cultural heritage of Hong Kong rests squarely, if somewhat uncomfortably, on the long and unique history of China. Within the Chinese *literati* tradition, much emphasis was placed on the acquisition and demonstration of skills such as brush painting, jade carving, furniture making and silk weaving, each of which took years to acquire. Today, the resulting artefacts are highly valued, aesthetically and commercially, and many have become 'collectors' items'. Some of the most desirable textiles are the highly ornate woven and embroidered Ming dynasty robes, or the popular 'Mandarin squares'.[9]

Traditionally, textiles were considered of cultural importance at ceremonies, festivals and in domestic life. Yards of red silk would be hung on the walls at wedding banquets as an auspicious sign to the marriage. Silk fabric can be regarded as a signifier of China itself, which, as its place of origin, has produced some of the finest-quality examples.

Many provinces in China are also renowned for textile folk crafts. In Suzhou and other cities in Jiangsu Province, where silkworms were raised, the embroidery skills of young women were perfected to a very high level. Poorer women produced folk embroidery as a way of contributing to the family income. To their more wealthy counterparts, embroidery was a pastime. They adorned their clothes and items for the home and gifts, such as small purses and pouches, with so-called 'boudoir embroidery'.[10] The skills continue today in local workshops. Similarly, in Henan Province in Central China, village women still continue to make traditional cloth toys.

Textiles have formed a particularly important part in the lives of China's 52 minority groups. The Miao people, who inhabit one of the country's poorest and more remote provinces, Guizhou, in the south west, are still involved with the whole process from the rearing of silkworms to the spinning, weaving, indigo dyeing and embroidery of the finished cloth. The resulting heavily decorated garments are no longer created simply for domestic necessity. They have been commoditised for the tourist and overseas markets.

Similarly, in the rural and fishing communities in Hong Kong, clothing and textile artefacts were traditionally made in the home for practical and symbolic reasons. Superstition had a particular influence on children's clothes which were embroidered and appliqued with flowers, animals and auspicious symbols to bring good fortune. Babies and infants wore special hats in the form of an animal such as a tiger, pig, or dog, with a face at the front and sometimes a padded tail at the back, to scare evil spirits or to fool them into thinking that the child was an animal. Shoes with bulging animal eyes were worn to prevent the child from tripping when learning to walk.[11]

Cloth baby carriers were the familiar means for mothers to transport their offspring on their backs while working in Hong Kong and southern China. The traditional carrier was made from a square of cloth with four long strips extending one from each corner to form straps. Along with the covers, which were worn over them in cold weather, they were embroidered and appliquéd with good luck symbols, traditionally by the child's grandmother. Nowadays, the land-dwelling Hakka and Punti (local Cantonese) people tend to buy factory-made traditional-style carriers, or modern Western ones. But hand-made versions can still be found amongst the more remote island-dwelling Tanka and Hoklo fishing communities.

The Hong Kong tailoring trade still relies on traditional skills, especially in the production of the hand-made *cheung sam*, or *qi bao*, the women's robe his-torically associated with Hong Kong. Their *huaniu*, or decorative handmade buttons and loops, were usually produced by women. But this highly skilled craft has virtually disappeared as part of a general decline in the trade.

Such textile crafts represent Chinese cultural heritage, signifying practices and traditional beliefs. But they are contrary to the image of progress and modernisation which Hong Kong people have wanted to project since the 1960s. Traditional practices and the associated material culture are seen as retrogressive. As more Asian communities aspire to late twentieth-century, Westernised life-styles, traditional crafts come under threat. The tourist mar-ket keeps craft skills alive, but in the process the resulting artefacts are liable to become fossilised as they cease to be part of living traditions. Indigenous people will prefer mass-produced equivalents, being relatively cheap, easily available, and, moreover, signifiers of modernity. Innovation can occur, as it has done in Japan and Korea, but for it to do so a cultural space must be prepared to receive and nurture it, one which welcomes the new, but equally values tradition.

One of the problems in Hong Kong is not only that local folk craft are undervalued, but that they are seen by many as an 'inherited tradition' originating in mainland China. As Abbas has pointed out, 'while 98% of the population is ethnic Chinese, history (both colonial history and history on the mainland) has seen to it that the Hong Kong Chinese are now culturally and politically quite distinct from mainlanders; two peoples separated by a common ethnicity'.[12] There is therefore some resistance to what is seen as mainland Chinese tradition by those seeking to effect a distinct Hong Kong cultural identity. Ironically, however, if the former British colony had not preserved certain traditions and festivals they would probably have disappeared completely as a casualty of the Cultural Revolution in China.

Since the late 1970s, Hong Kong has begun to develop its own cultural dynamic. So far, this has been evident mainly in popular culture and the massmedia, notably in the local film and television industries. In the 1990s some local writers and critics began to generate a local cultural studies narrative, initially by applying Western cultural theory to Hong Kong. But in order to generate its own contemporary cultural production, Hong Kong needs to establish a space which can facilitate the new and also create local confidence in what is generated in the territory.

Textile Design and Mass-Production

Since the establishment of the first cotton spinning and weaving factories in the 1950s, textiles have been a mainstay of Hong Kong's manufacturing industry. The migration of Shanghai textile entrepreneurs had a significant effect on the development of the local industry. Their business commitment and determination was underpinned by capital, modern machinery and advanced technology. Manufacturing was further stimulated by the crisis of the political changes in China and a collapse of the *entrepot* trade triggered by the Korean War and the United Nations trade embargo with China.[13] Labour-intensive light consumer industries, especially textiles and clothing, were major sectors for development in the 1950s and 1960s.

By the late 1970s Hong Kong was the developed world's leading exporter of mass-produced textiles and clothing. But with the opening up of China to foreign direct investment, manufacturing began to move from Hong Kong to southern China where labour and land costs were cheaper. Hong Kong's manufacturing industry was export-oriented from the outset and so it continued. As a result, textile manufacturing developed on the 'OEM' (own equipment manufacture) model, a process whereby designs were supplied by the overseas client, rather than being generated in Hong Kong. Therefore, there was no demand for textile design, either for the local or foreign markets. But the movement of textile manufacturing to places with cheaper labour, such as mainland China, Indonesia, Malaysia, Thailand and the Philippines, may have positive effects on the production of textile design in Hong Kong. A number of local textile manufactures are attempting to remain competitive by moving up-market into value-added merchandise with original designs.[14]

The issue of establishing a local identity troubles not only the manufacturing industry, but also individuals, especially those involved in cultural production, and in the visual arts.

Hong Kong Visual Art

Western influence has been highly influential on the development of the visual arts in Hong Kong, in tandem with classical forms of Chinese painting. They have been successfully integrated into new visual vocabularies by artists such as Wucius Wong, or Kan Tai Keung. But such developments have not strayed beyond the boundaries of fine arts conventions, and have often depended on the instigation of key individuals. Western ideas and techniques, therefore, have tended to come either from foreigners resident in Hong Kong or from the returning diaspora. On the positive side, this kept the territory in touch with the international art world, but it also privileged some forms of practice, and excluded others. In this context contemporary textile art would almost be viewed as 'alternative practice', especially bearing in mind its associations with female practitioners and the domestic environment. It does not form part of the mainstream, nor is it preferred by galleries or art collectors. But then one local artist has suggested that all art in Hong Kong can be seen as 'alternative':

> Though Hong Kong has sophistication in many and numerous ways, art is never considered as essential nor given any real importance. In many cases, artworks are regarded and appreciated more for their decorative attributes or meticulous craft and execution. ...[O]ur museums and art centres, institutions are as marginalised as those labeled 'alternative', ...in effect, art in Hong Kong, as for the public, is realistically all 'alternative'.[15]

In Hong Kong art is seen as a commodity, purchased for investment. Commercial galleries, and the local art institutions, tend to favour the foreign, the famous, and current market trends.[16] This, I would argue, has had a stultifying effect on local creative practice. There are few venues for public exhibition, therefore local artists must court public and commercial galleries in order to receive exposure. But the same galleries consider Hong Kong artists of marginal interest when compared with outsiders. Modern Western artists are favoured, especially those with an established reputation and a 'name'. In the 1990s, contemporary realist painting from mainland China and Taiwan began to catch the commercial limelight and command high prices. Art which combined a political edge and employed Western visual language, proved particularly attractive to international buyers. While some older generation Hong Kong artists can make a living from their work, galleries are not willing to take commercial risks on the less well known.[17]

This is symptomatic of the fact that Hong Kong does not have confidence in its own; external approbation is required as validation. Responsibility can be laid at the door of colonialism having undermined the self- confidence of Hong Kong in its people, products and practice. Such insecurity influences all cultural practice. Within the gallery system, definitions of what constitutes 'real art' remain very conventional. To enter the system, local practitioners must abide by existing protocol, both in the media and content of their work. Simply speaking, if local galleries do not show textile art, then artists courting the galleries will not be inclined to produce it. Textile art, where it exists in Asia (such as in Japan), has been effected by the amalgamation of indigenous tradition and contemporary innovation. In Hong Kong this is only starting to happen.

Interesting developments took place in the 1990s, when younger artists started to make installations, an art form then essentially new to Hong Kong. Site-specific work removed itself from the strictures of the art institution, into the community. It was documented and then disappeared, but in the process it came to signify the existence of a Hong Kong *avant-garde*, unafraid to experiment with media or ideas and independent of the gallery system. Key in this movement was Para-Site, a group of installation artists, established in 1996 by Kith Tang, Tak-ping, and Warren Leung in the old Western district on Hong Kong island. They wanted to evoke a local consciousness, which was characterised by a concern with issues of personal and collective identity, and memory. Traditional Chinese icons and items of material culture, including textiles, were incorporated into their work, especially by Tsang.

Kith Tsang spent his childhood in the old Western district, an area which has preserved some Chinese folk traditions and artefacts longer than the more modernised areas of the city.18 He evokes former times by including found 'memory' objects in his pieces. In Part 4 of his 'Hello! Hong Kong' installation series, staged at Rennie's Mill, [19] he hung lengths of fabric across the frames of old rusty bunk beds. The cheap printed fabrics which are commonplace in the Hong Kong Chinese home achieved his intention, of giving 'a family look to the structure'.[20] These simple pieces of cloth demonstrated the evocative power of even the most unostentatious textiles

During the handover period Tsang was optimistic that a much needed art discourse would be established in Hong Kong. But this did not take place mainly, he feels, because most local artists are too immature to respond to one another's work or to the past. A lack of a sense of tradition in Hong Kong has inspired Para-Site to try to engender a local consciousness amongst artists. Tsang makes comparisons with Taiwan, where he sees the visual arts as being more developed and sophisticated.[21] Local critic David Clarke echoes his view:

> Not only does Hong Kong lack any high cultural tradition of its
> own which can serve as resource, it also lacks support from either
> an ethnic or a national narrative in a broader sense... Hong Kong
> identity can only be expressed in art as a trace, as a species of
> nonessentialist, unrooted, post-modern identity.[22]

The lack of recognition of an indigenous culture in Hong Kong sets it apart
from neighbouring developed countries like Taiwan, South Korea and Japan
(each having established it own contemporary textile art practice).

The development of installation art acted as a 'great liberation' for many
young Hong Kong artists of the 1990s as it enabled them to make big pieces
in a short time and opened up an unlimited range of materials.[23] The inclusion
of objects of everyday life expanded the visual vocabulary and encouraged
a sensitivity towards material culture. But it was also, 'a fast food culture...
hastily put together, changing in form and content rapidly and designed for
immediate consumption rather than for lengthy digestion and sustained investigation.'[24]

The fault was not entirely that of the artists, but reflective of Hong Kong's
urban lifestyle and ingrained obsession with materialism.[25] Local exhibitions
usually rely on finance from the exhibitor's own pocket. As a result they
tend to run for a matter of days, and receive relatively little exposure. The
Hong Kong Arts Development Council (HKADC) is the only public source
of financial support. It has enabled artists, such as those involved in Para-
Site, to take their work into the community and to appropriate alternative
spaces. But its funds are inevitably limited and subject to competition. There
is relatively little public support for innovation in culture and the arts. As
noted earlier, this is, typicaly, attributed to the colonial situation which has
concentrated the energy of the place on the development of the economy.
Therefore, many artists who have gained the confidence to negotiate new
and individual forms of creative practice have been part of the diaspora.

Hong Kong Textile Artists

Kai Chan is a Canadian textile artist who has gained international recognition [see colour plate no. 14]. Born in China, Chan moved to Hong Kong
with his family as a young boy in 1949, following the Japanese invasion. In
1966 they emigrated to Canada, where Chan then made his home. He recalls
that his first conscious encounter with his ethnic identity was in Canada.

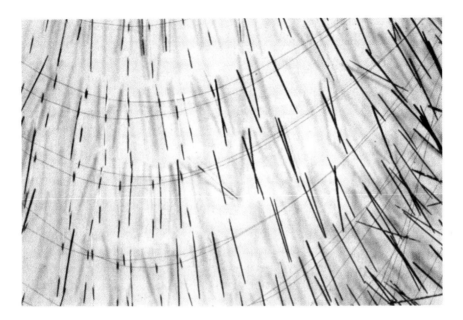

Kai Chan
Veil, Light, Cat's Eye, Net (1995) (detail)
toothpick, thread, nail
131 x 90 x 6cm 3 / 8 / 99

The Hong Kong of his youth was very colonial, with a dearth of Chinese artefacts. Ironically, he had to search Canadian libraries and museums to find out about 'being Chinese'.[26]

His initial interest in textile art was inspired by an exhibition, *Wall Hanging*, at the Museum of Modern Art, New York, in 1969. He admires Western techniques of painting and sculpture, but sees them as foreign. Natural materials and a love of artefacts made by indigenous peoples are what inspire him. Textiles are his point of connection with the traditional Chinese material world of fabrics, wood, bamboo and paper. He uses thread and wood, and painted toothpicks to create delicate textile hangings and also bold pieces of jewellery. Natural materials are carefully integrated to give the works a delicate quality, almost vergmg on the mystical. The pieces have a deceptive simplicity. As one commentator has observed: .

> It seems to be about poetics... Some of his most intricate structures result in the simplest of forms... Sometimes, what seems to be a mute gesture in his work continues to speak to me long after I have left the piece, *haiku* lodged in my brain, except it has no words.[27]

Chan's work is not autobiographical, but he recognises that his experiences have dictated his way of seeing and interpreting the world. While he prefers to forget his early life in Hong Kong and China, he nevertheless identifies himself, ethnically and culturally, as 'Chinese'. This is reflected in the sensitivity of his work, his materials and his methods. To Western eyes they have an 'otherness', reflected in a lightness and fragility which recalls Zen emptiness.

Another textile artist, Chan Suet Fun also originated in Hong Kong, but moved to the Netherlands in 1983. Her work is essentially different from Kai Chan's, but they share the common fact of their overseas experience having been implicit to their becoming textile artists. Suet Fun went abroad to develop her creativity and her fascination with textiles which, at the time, she found impossible to do in Hong Kong due to the conservativeness of the visual arts and limited educational opportunities. She studied costume design, then textile design at the Academy of Visual Art, in Maastricht. On graduation she rented a subsidised studio from the local council, which enable her to practise, as an artist and a teacher. Many of her ideas are inspired by her cultural background and Chinese ethnicity. They have been developed through a range of materials and techniques, which have included experiments with screen printing, silk painting, collage, soft sculpture, and paper construction.

A grant from the HKADC supported her first one-person show in the SAR late in 1998. It is her intention to return to Hong Kong, where recently she has run courses on textile art for the Hong Kong Museum of Art. However, she acknowledges that, in Asia, textile practice lags behind the rest of the world. She attributes this to a historical lack of concern for cultural and creative development and a lack of educational opportunity. Despite positive changes in the 1990s, she also recognises the difficulties of merely existing as a textile artist in Hong Kong. But her desire to do so and to educate others could be significant in helping to develop new media and ideas.

Currently there is only one, quite traditional, Fine Art course in Hong Kong's seven universities, and no courses devoted exclusively to textile design. The reason is pragmatic. Historically, the Hong Kong government encouraged vocational courses in the institutions it funded, to service the local manufacturing industries. Textiles were produced in the colony, but the designs were not. There was no apparent need, therefore, for textile design education.[28] Today, fashion design is offered at degree level, along with clothing and textile marketing and product studies; all are based on Western models, are industry focused and provide little space for alternative or hybrid developments. As Rey Chow has noted, Hong Kong is

...like everywhere else in the 'developing' world, already predis-posed toward vocational and technical training. Traditional culture, having lost its power to intervene politically since the preconditions for that power have disappeared, takes on an ornamental function in the form of museum masterpieces.[29]

In any attempt at re-orienting textile practice, or the fine arts, towards textile art, education is a key issue. But so too is indigenous culture which must be afforded a space within contemporary life. Tradition and innovation should not be seen as oppositional, for by being conjoined, often unexpectedly, the new can begin to emerge.

Evidence of contemporary innovation by young Chinese artists was il-lustrated in an exhibition staged in Hong Kong and Taipei early in 1998 titled *New Voices: Contemporary Art from Hong Kong, Taipei and Shanghai*. The prevailing concerns were identified as, 'Personal language', 'Being women', 'Identity through history', 'Technology and possibilities', and 'The search for something Chinese'.[30] Two women exhibited forms of 'textile art'.

Taiwanese artist Liu Chu-Liang[31] explored female consciousness with her mixed media works, including her small triptych, 'If I am him, she is me, but she is not me, I am not him' (1995). An elongated female, simply framed in her own glass case, was flanked on one side by a dancer and on the other by an ornate shoe, isolated at the centre of a triangle. The surfaces were soft and colourless, as is characteristic of Liu's work which uses cloth, fibre, cotton and other materials which relate to the human body. Her themes are drawn from the familiar, from within her own environment. She sees herself as part of an established practice in Taiwan, where contemporary female artists like Wang Li-kuen, Wang Wen-yin, and Tsu Suen-wei use textiles as a medium to explore their self-experience.[32]

Similar concerns about 'being women' are shared by young Hong Kong artist Phoebe Man, Ching-ying who also exhibited in the New Voices show [see colour plate no. 15]. Her work provides evidence of change in the Hong Kong visual arts which reveals a new hybridity or the emergence of Bhab-ha's 'Third Space'. Man creates forms using a variety of mixed media.[33] In her first solo show in 1994, *I Eat Therefore I Am*, she used various traditional Chinese foods such as rice, noodles, and salt fish, as well as margarine, to create her 'Rice Bed, Rice Fruit Sandwich and Margarine Wall'. Two years later she began her 'Beautiful Flowers' series as a way of investigating fe-male reproduction and menstruation, subjects which remain taboo in Hong Kong. Simple, soft flowers were constructed from disposable paper sanitary napkins and then combined into soft sculptural forms. Some of the 'red eggs' (symbolising birth) at the centres of the flowers appeared to be leaking and staining the pure white petals. One of the pieces was included in the *New Voices* show. Man eschews the title 'feminist artist' because she feels that her work is insufficiently grounded in theory. But she is committed to exploring ideas and media. She criticises the lack of innovation in much Hong Kong art since the 1960s, describing it as 'art for art's sake', lacking in content.

Many Hong Kong artists are searching for a voice which can reflect the complexities of their own cultural identity. Just as conventional identity labels, such as 'Chinese' or 'British', are limited, the use of traditional 'Western' or 'Chinese' media only highlights the inadequacies of each. While the Hong Kong diaspora have been able to engage with the established conventions of textile art, this is not so for local artists. For the postcolonial identity can only be articulated in a new space, a space of hybridity. This space is beginning to be craeated by artists such as Kith Tsang, Phoebe Man, and by Para-Site. By looking to tradition, not as static or inferior, but as alive and of contemporary relevance, a space is being created for new forms to emerge. This is the point at which Hong Kong begins to re-define itself on its own terms. The outcome may not be instantly classifiable, or recognisable to outsiders, but will emerge as a hybrid form. As Ackbar Abbas has pointed out, the problem with the question of postcolonial identity in Hong Kong can no longer take its bearings from old binarisms (like the difference between 'East' and 'West', 'tradition' and 'modernity'):

> What is both culturally and politically more important is the development of a new Hong Kong subjectivity, that is, subjectivity constructed not narcissistically but in the very process of negotiating the mutations and permutations of colonialism, nationalism, and capitalism.[34]

If 'textile art' is to emerge in Hong Kong, it will be as a new and hybrid form, one which acknowledges tradition, but does not fear innovation. It is already evident that such work will not stay within previously prescribed boundaries.

Notes

1.   Presented by Hong Kong Land Group Limited, The Rotunda, Exchange Square, 23 August – 25 September 1994.
2.   *Newsletter of the Textile Society of Hong Kong*, vol. 2, no. 5, 15 October 1994, p. 4.
3 .   Rey Chow, *Writing Diaspora: Tactics of Intervention in Contemporary Cultural Studies*, 1993, p. 23.

4. Tsang Yok Sing, 'Arts People Ruling the Arts', *Straight Talk: a collection of essays on Hong Kong affairs*, 1995, p. 24.

5. Ackbar Abbas, *Hong Kong, Culture and the Politics of Disappearance*, Hong Kong University Press, Hong Kong, 1997, p. 2.

6. Han Suyin's much repeated phrase is noted, amongst others, by Abbas, 1997, p. 142.

7. Abbas, op cit, 1997, p. 6

8. Homi K. Bhabha, 'Cultural Diversity and Cultural Differences', in Bill Ashcroft, Gareth Griffiths and Helen Tiffin (eds), *The Post-Colonial Studies Reader*, Routledge, London, 1993, p. 209.

9. A common name for the 'rank badges' used to identify officials, especially in the Ming and Qing dynasties.

10. Qiu Huanxing, *Folk Customs of China*, Foreign Languages Press, Beijing, 1992, p. 60.

11. Naomi, Yin-yin, Szeto & Valery M. Garrett, *Children of the Gods, Dress and Symbolism in China*, Urban Council, Hong Kong, 1990, p. 78 & p. 30.

12. Ackbar Abbas, op.cit., 1997, p. 2.

13. Suzanne Berger and Richard K. Lester, *Made By Hong Kong*, Oxford University Press, Hong Kong, 1997, p. 19.

14. Sung Yun-wing & Lee Ming-kwan, *The Other Hong Kong Report 1991*, The Chinese University Press, Hong Kong, 1991, p. 190.

15. Warren Leung, *Para/Site 1996*, Para/Site, Hong Kong, 1996, pp. 6–7.

16. This was exemplified by the opening exhibition at the new Hong Kong Museum of Art, in 1991. *Too French*, an exhibition of contemporary French art, was devoid of any local cultural significance.

17. Established artists would include painter Wucius Wong and sculptor Van Lau.

18. One is the so-called 'singing dragon boat', in which an individual performer, carrying a stick with a model dragon boat on top, is invited in by shops to sing in a local colloquial manner. Only one performer now remains in the Sheung Wan district.

19. An isolated residential area of Kowloon, now no longer occupied, which kept strong ties with the Chinese Nationalists and Taiwan.

20. Kith Tsang, *Hello! Hong Kong: Analysis of Exhibited Works*, unpublished essay, Hong Kong, August 1997, p. 28.

21. Interview with Kith Tsang, Tak-ping, 16 March 1998.

22. David Clarke, 'Between East and West: Negotiations with Tradition and Modernity in Hong Kong Art', *Art and Place*, Hong Kong University Press, Hong Kong, 1996, p. 76.

23. Oscar Ho, 'Installation: New Possibilides, New Crises', Private Content: Public View, compiled by Eric Otto Wear and Lisa Cheung, Hong Kong Festival Fringe, 1997, p.18.

24. *Ibid*., 1997, p. 20.

25. Nyaw Mee-kau and Li Si-ming, *The Other Hong Kong Report 1996*, The Chinese University of Hong Kong, 1996, p. 475: comment, 'it is indisputable that Hong Kong is a materialistic society'.

26. Kai Chan: *In Search of Paradise*, exhibihon catalogue, The Library and Gallery, Cambridge, Ontario, Canada, October 27 – December 1, 1996, p. 9.

27. J. R. Carpenter, *Kai Chan*, 1996, p. 15.

28. The Chinese University of Hong Kong offers degree and graduate studies in Fine Art, and The Hong Kong Polytechnic University offers degree courses in fashion design, and textile and clothing studies, but not in textile design.

29. Rey Chow, op.cit., 1993, p. 136–137.

30. Oscar Ho, 'Hong Kong: Looking for Something', *New Voices: Contemporary Art from Hong Kong, Taipei and Shanghai,* Pao Galleries, Hong Kong Arts Centre, and Zhung Zheng Gallery, National Taiwan Arts Education Institute, 1998.

31. Liu Chu-Liang was born in Kaohshiung, Taiwan, in 1966, and graduated from The National Academy of Arts, Taiwan, in 1997. She commenced a graduate course in the Plastic Arts Department of the Taiwan National College of the Arts.

32. Liu Chu-Liang, letter to the author, dated 6 May 1998.
33. Phoebe Man acknowledges the influence of her tutor at the Chinese University of Hong Kong, Chan Yuk-keung, who returned to teach at his *alma mater* after a Masters course at Cranbrook Academy in the United States. He has a subtle, intellectual approach to his sculpture which often incorporates found objects to explore cultural and political issues.
34. Abbas, op.cit., 1997, p. 11.

BIBLIOGRAPHY

Abbas, A., *Hong Kong, Culture and the Politics of Disappearance*, Hong Kong University Press, Hong Kong, 1997.

Albers, A., *On Designing*, Wesleyan University Press, Connecticut, 1961.

Anscombe, I., *A Woman's Touch: Women in Design from 1860 to the Present Day*, Virago, London, 1984.

Appadurai, A. (ed.), *The Social Life of Things: Commodities in Cultural Perspectives*, Cambridge University Press, Urne, 1997.

Ashcroft, B., Griffiths, G. and Tiffin H. (eds), *The Post-Colonial Studies Reader*, Routledge, London, 1993.

Bachmann, I. and Scheuing, R. (eds), *Material Matters: The Art and Culture of Contemporary Textiles*, YYZBooks, Canada, 1998.

Barber, E. J. W., *Prehistoric Textiles: the development of cloth in the Neolithic and Bronze ages, with special reference to the Aegean*, Princeton University Press, New Jersey, 1990.

Barringer, T. and Flynn, T. (eds), *Colonialism and the Object: Empire, Material Culture and the Museum*, Routledge, London and New York, 1998.

Bartlet, P., 'Rugs R Us (and them): the Oriental carpet as sign and text', *Third Text*, vol.30, 1995.

Bell, D., *Daughters of the Dreaming*, Mc Phee Gribble/George Allen and Unwin, Melbourne, 1993.

Berger, S. and Lester, R.K., *Made By Hong Kong*, Oxford University Press, Hong Kong, 1997.

Berman, M., *All That is Solid Melts into Air*, Simon and Schuster, New York, 1982.

Berman, M., *Todo lo sólido se desvanece en el aire*, Siglo XXI, Madrid, 1988.

Bertens, H., *The idea of the Postmodern: A History*, Routledge, London and New York, 1995.

Bhabba, H. *The Location of Culture*, London and New York, Routledge, 1994.

Bieber, M., *The History of Greek and Roman Theatre*, Princeton University Press, Princeton NJ, 1961.

Blinkenberg, C., *Les Petits Objets, Lindos: Les fouilles de l'Acropole 1902–1914*, Walter de Gruyter, Berlin, 1931.

Briggs, A., *Victorian Things*, Penguin, London, 1988.

Brockensha, P., *The Pitjantjatjara and their Crafts*, Aboriginal Arts Board, Australia Council, Sydney, 1975.

Brody, A., *Utopia A Picture Story*, ex. cat., Tandanya National Aboriginal Cultural Institute, Adelaide, 1989.

Bröhan, T. and Berg, T., *Avantgarde Design 1880–1930*, Taschen, Koln, 1995.

Bryson, N., *Looking at the Overlooked: Four Essays on Still Life Paintings*, Reaktion Books, London, 1990.

Budick, S. and Iser, W. (eds), *The Translatability of Cultures: Figurations of the Space Between*, Stanford University Press, Stanford, California, 1996.

Burger, P., *Theory of Avant-Garde*, University of Minnesota Press, Minneapolis, 1984.

Burger, P., *Teoría de la Vaguarida (The Theory of the Avant-Garde)*, Peninsula, Barcelona, 1987.

Calabrese, O., *Cómo se lee una Obra de Arte*, Cátedra, Sogno e Imagen, Madrid, 1994.

Calasso, R., *The Marriage of Cadmus and Harmony* (trans. Tim Parkes), Vintage, Sydney, 1994.

Carter, M., *Putting a Face on Things: Studies in Imaginary Materials*, Power Institute, Sydney, 1997.

Cassiman, B. (ed), *The Sublime Void: on the memory of the imagination*, ex. cat, Koninklijk Museum, Antwerp, 1993.

Chambers, I. and Curti, L. (eds), *The Post-Colonial Reader: Common Skies, Divided Horizons*, Routledge, London, 1996.

Chavane, M., 'Les Petits Objects', *Salamine de Chypre*, vol vi. Diffusion de Boccard, Paris 1975.

Chow, R., *Writing Diaspora: Tactics of Intervention in Contemporary Cultural Studies*, Bloomington: Indiana University Press, Indiana, 1993.

Chruszczyñska, J., *Makaty buczackie w zbiorach Museum Narodowego w Warszawie. Tapestries from Buczacz in the collection of the National Museum in Warsaw*, Warszawa, 1996 (in Polish and English).

Clark, J., *Modern Asian Art*, Craftsman House, Sydney, 1998.

Clarke, D., 'East and West: Negotiations with Tradition and Modernity in Hong Kong Art', *Art And Place*, Hong Kong University Press, Hong Kong, 1996.

Clifford, J., Routes: *Travel and Translation in the Late Twentieth Century*, Harvard University Press, Cambridge and London, 1997.

Clifford, J., *Dilemas de la Cultura*, Gedisa, Barcelona, 1995.

Clifford, J., *The Predicament of Culture*, The President and Fellows of Harvard College, USA, 1988.

Cochrane, G., *The Crafts Movement in Australia: A History*, UNSW Press, Sydney, 1992.

Collins, M., *Towards Postmodernism: Design Since 1851*, British Museum Publications, London, 1987.

Colomina, B. (ed.), *Sexuality and Space*, Princeton Papers on Architecture, Princeton University School of Architecture, New Jersey, 1992.

Cygan. Only Textiles. New Old Works, ex. cat., The City Galleries in Lodz, May–June 1998.

Danto, A., 'Art and Artifact in Africa', *Inside the Brillo Box*, Farrar, Straus Giroux, New York, 1992.

Davidson, G. R., 'Minor Objects', *Corinth*, vol xii, American School of Classical Studies at Athens, Princeton NJ, 1952.

de Certeau, M., *The Practice of Everyday Life* (trans L. Stephen Rendall), University of California Press, Berkeley, 1988.

Debord, G., *La sociedad del espectaculo (The Performance Society)*, La Marca, Buenos Aires, 1995.

Demos C., *Kourion: its monuments and local museum*, Andros Pavlides, Nicosia Cyprus, 1996.

Dormer, P. (ed.), *The Culture of Craft: Status and Future*, Manchester University Press, Manchester and New York, 1997.

Douglas, M., *The Craftsman as Yeoman: Myth and Cultural Identity in American Craft*, Haystack Monograph series, Deer Isle, ME, 1995.

Elkin, A. P., *The Australian Aborigines: how to understand them*, Angus and Robertson, Sydney, (1943) 1961.

Fisher, J. (ed.), *Global Visions: Towards a New Internationalism in the Visual Arts*, Kala Press, London, 1994.

Forty, A., *Objects of Desire: Design and Society 1750–1980*, Thames and Hudson, London, 1987.

Frickiewicz, H. (ed.), *Splódzieluia Artystów LAD. 1926-1996 [Artists' Co-Operative LAD (Order). 1926–1996]*, Warszawa, 1998 (in Polish and English). See Chapter II 'Textiles': Halina Jurga, 'Kilims, Tapestries, Carpets'; Hubert Bilewicz, 'Jacquard Loom Fabrics at Lad'; Anna Demska, 'Lad and Folk Weaving Tradition – the Work of Eleonora Plutynska'; Anna Demska, 'Lad Painted and Printed Fabrics'. See also: Anna Frickiewicz, 'Lad: The Cridcal Perspective'; Irena Huml, 'The Lad Cooperative: Background, Philosophy and Programme'

Frascina, F., *Pollock and After: The Critical Debate*, Harper & Row, London, 1985.

Friedland, R. and Boden, D. (eds), *Now Here: Space, Time and Modernity*, University of California Press, Berkeley, Los Angeles and London, 1994.

Gablik, S., *Conversations Before the End of Time*, Thames and Hudson, London, 1995.

Gablik, S., *Has Modernism Failed?*, Thames and Hudson, London, 1994.

García Canclini, N., *Hybrid Cultures: Strategies for Entering and Leaving Modernity*, University of Minnesota Press, Minneapolis, 1995.

Gilborn, C., *Adirondack Furniture and the Rustic Tradition*, Harry N. Abrams, New York, 1987.

Gleason, A., Kenez, P. and Stites, R., *Bolshevik Culture: Experiment and Order in the Russion Revolution*, Indiana University Press, Bloomington and Indianapolis, 1985.

Green, J., *Utopia: Women, Country and Batik*, Utopia Women's Batik Group, Alice Springs, 1981.

Guilbaut, S., *De como Nueva York robó la idea de arte moderno (How New York Stole the Idea of Modern Art)*, Mondadori, Madrid, 1990.

Gulberg, E. and Astrom, P., 'The thread of Ariadne: a study in ancient Greek dress', *Studies in Mediterranean Archaeology*, XXI, Goteborg, Sweden, 1970.

Hall, J., *Dictionary of Subjects and Symbols in Art*, John Murray, London 1984.

Hamby, L., and Mellor, D., 'Fibre Tracks', *Oxford Companion to Aboriginal Art and Culture* (eds Kleinert, S. and Neale, M.), Oxford University Press, Melbourne, 1999.

Harrison, C., *Modernism*, Tate Gallery Publishing, London, 1997.

Hemming, S., 'Aboriginal Coiled Basketry in South Australia', *Journal of the Anthropological Society of South Australia*, July 1989, pp. 48–50.

Ho, O., 'Hong Kong: Looking for Something', *New Voices: Contemporary Art from Hong Kong, Taipei and Shanghai*, Pao Galleries, Hong Kong Arts Centre, and Zhung Zheng Gallery, National Taiwan Arts Educahon Institute, 1998.

Ho, O., 'Installation: New Possibilities, New Crises', *Private Content: Public View*, compiled by Eric Otto Wear & Lisa Cheung, Hong Kong Festival Fringe, 1997.

Hobsbawn, E. and Ranger, T. (eds), *The Invention of Tradition*, Cambridge University Press, Cambridge, New York and Melbourne, 1997 [1983].

Hoskins, J., Biographical Objects: *How Things Tell the Stories of People's Lives*, Routledge, New York and London, 1998.

Howes, D. (ed), *Cross-Cultural Consumption: Global Markets, Local Realities*, Routledge, London and New York, 1996.

Huanxing, Q., *Folk Customs of China*, Foreign Languages Press, Beijing, 1992.

Huml, I., *Polska Tkanina Wsp – Iczesna (Polish Contemporary Tapestry]*, Warszawa, 1989 (in Polish only).

Huml, I., *Warsztaty Krakowskie* [Cracow Workshops], Wroclaw, Warszawa, Kraków, Gdańsk, 1973 (in Polish only).

Hutcheon, L., *The Politics of Postmodernism*, Routledge, London and New York, 1989.

Hutcheon, L., *A Poetics of Postmodernism: History, Theory*, London and New York, 1988.

Huyssen, A., *After the Great Divide: Modernism, Mass Culture, Postmodernism*, Indiana University Press, Bloomington and Indianapolis, 1986.

Huyssen, A., *Twilight Memories: Marking Time in a Culture of Amnesia*, Routledge, New York and London, 1995.

Isaacs, J., *The Gentle Arts: 200 Years of Australian Women's Domestic and Decorative Arts*, Lansdowne, Willoughby, New South Wales, 1987.

Jackson, J. B., *A Sense of Place, a Sense of Time*, Yale University Press, New Haven, 1994.

Jacobs, M. J., 'Anni Albers: A Modern Weaver as Artist,' *The Woven and Graphic Art of Anni Albers*, Smithsonian Press, Washington, D.C., 1985.

Jain, J. (ed.), *Other Masters: Five Contemporary Folk and Tribal Artists of India*, Crafts Museum and The Handicrafts and Handlooms Exports Corporation of India, New Delhi, 1998.

Kai Chan: In Search of Paradise, exhibition catalogue, The Library and Gallery, Cambridge, Ontario, Canada, 27 October – 1 December 1996.

Kearney, R., *The Wake of Imagination: Ideas of Creativity in Western Culture*, Hutchinson, London, Melbourne, Auckland & Johannesburg, 1988.

Kerenyi, C. E., *Archetypal image of mother and daughter* (trans. Mannheim, R.), Princeton University Press, Princeton New Jersey, 1991.

Kerr, J. (ed.), *Heritage: The National Women's Art Book*, Art & Australia, Sydney, 1995.

Krauss, R. E., *The Originality of the Avant-Garde and Other Modernist Myths*, The MIT Press, Cambridge and London, 1987.

Lavie, S., Narayan, K., and Rosaldo, R. (eds) *Creativity/Anthropology*, Cornell University Press, Ithaca and London, 1993.

Lefkowitz, M. R. and Fant, M. B., *Women's Life in Greece and Rome,* Duckworth, Great Britain, 1992.

Leung, W., *Para/Site 1996*, Para/Site Art Space, Hong Kong, 1996.

Lippard, L. (ed.), *Mapping the Terrain: New Genre Public Art*, Bay Press, Seattle, 1995.

Logan, J., 'Towards a definition of Australian folk art', ex. cat., *Everyday Art: Australian Folk Art*, National Gallery of Australia, Canberra, 1998.

Lubar, S., and Kingery, W. D. (eds) *History from Things: Essays on Material Culture*, Smithsonian Institudon Press, Washington and London, 1993.

Maharaj, S., 'Arachne's Genre: Towards Inter-Cultural Studies in Textiles', *Journal of Design History*, vol. 4, no. 2, Oxford: Oxford University Press 1991, pp. 75–96.

Maningrida: the language of weaving, ex. cat. Australian Exhibitions Touring Agency, Melbourne, 1995.

Marinatos, N. and Hagg, R. (eds), *Greek sanctuaries: New approaches*, Routledge, London and New York, 1993

Marx, L., *The Machine in the Garden*, Oxford University Press, New York, 1967.

McCracken, G., 'Many Voices', *Many Voices: 13th Tamworth Fibre Textile Biennial*, ex. cat., Tamworth City Gallery, Tamworth, New South Wales, 1998.

McCullough, M., *Abstracting Craft: The Practiced Digital Hand*, The MIT Press, Cambridge and London, 1996.

McLean, I., *White Aborigines: Identity Politics in Australian Art*, Cambridge University Press, Cambridge, New York and Melbourne, 1998.

McNamara, A. and Snelling, P., *Design and Practice for Printed Textiles*, Oxford University Press, Melbourne, 1995.

Mellor, D., 'Exploring the dynamics of surface and origin: Australian Indigenous textile and fibre practice', *Origins and New Perspectives – Contemporary Australian Textiles* (ed. King, G.), ex. cat., *9th International Trienniale of Tapestry*, Lódz, Poland 1998, Queen Victoria Museum and Art Gallery and Craft Australia, Launceston, Tasmania, 1998.

Mellor, D., 'Indigenous Australian Dyed and Printed Textiles', *Artlink*, February 1997.

Menz, C., *Objects from the Dreaming*, ex. cat., Art Gallery of South Australia, Adelaide, 1996.

Mercer, K., 'Art That Is Ethnic In Inverted Commas: on Yinka Shonibare, *Frieze* 35, Nov. /Dec. 1995, pp. 38–41.

Mercer, K., 'Back to my routes: A postscript to the 80s', ex. cat., *Pictura Britannica Art from Britain*, Museum of Contemporary Art, Sydney, 1997.

Miller, D., *Material Cultures: Why Some Things Matter*, UCL Press, London, 1998.

Modelski T. (ed.), *Studies in Entertainment: Critical Approaches to Mass Culture*, University of Indiana Press, Bloomington, 1986.

Morris, S., 'From Modernism to manure, perspectives on Classical Archaeology', *Antiquity*, vol. 69, no. 262, 1995, pp. 182–185.

Nicolaou, K., 'Excavations at Nea Paphos: The House of Dionysos, outline of the campaigns 1964–65', *Report of the Department of Antiquities in Cyprus*, Department of Antiquities, Nicosia, Cyprus, 1967, pp.100–125.

Novak, B., *Nature and Culture*, Oxford University Press, New York, 1980.

Osborne, P, *The Politics of Time: Modernity and Avant Garde*, Verso, London New York, 1995

Papastergiadis, N. (ed.), *Annotations 1, Mixed Belongings and Unspecified Destinations*, Institute of International Visual Arts, London, 1996.

Parker, R. and Pollock, G., *Old Mistresses, Women, Art and Ideology*, Routledge & Kegan Paul, London, 1981.

Paz, O., *Convergences: Essays on Art and Literature* (transl. Lane, H.), Bloomsbury, London, 1990.

Pearce, S. M. (ed.), *Experiencing Material Culture in the Western World*, Leicester University Press, London and Washington, 1997.

Perkins, H. (ed.), *Fluent. La Biennale di Venezia 1997. Australia*, ex cat. (ed..), Art Gallery of New South Wales, Sydney, 1997.

Phelan, P., *Mourning Sex; Performing Public Memories*, Routledge, London and New York, 1997.

Picton, J. (ed.), *The Art of African Textiles: Technology, Tradition and Lurex*, ex. cat., Lund Humphries and Barbican Art Gallery, London, 1995.

Rabinowitz, N. S. and Richlin, A. (eds), *Feminist Theory and the Classics*, Routledge, New York, 1993.

Robinson, G. and Rundell, J. (eds), *Rethinking Imagination: Culture and Creativity*, Routledge, London and New York, 1994.

Rowley S. (ed.), *Craft and Contemporary Theory*, Allen and Unwin, Sydney, 1997.

Rowley, S., *Crossing Borders: Contemporary Australian Textile Art*, ex. cat., University of Wollongong, Wollongong, 1995.

Schama S. *Landscape and Memory*, Fontana, London, 1996.

Schneid, J. and Svenbro, J., *The Craft of Zeus: myths of weaving and fabric*, Harvard University Press, Cambridge, Mass. 1996.

Schor, N., *Reading in Detail: Aesthetics and the Feminine*, Methuen, London, 1987.

Sing, T. Y., 'Arts People Ruling the Arts', *Straight Talk: a collection of essays on Hong Kong affairs*, Heaven and Earth Books Co. Ltd., Hong Kong, 1995.

Sontag, S., *A Susan Sontag Reader* (introd. Hardwick, E.), Penguin, London, 1992.

Soren, D. and James, J., *Kourion, the search for a lost Roman city*, Doubleday, New York and London, 1988.

Stein, G., *Picasso*, Beacon Press, Boston, 1959.

Suleiman, S. R. (ed.), *Exile and Creativity: Signposts, Travellers, Outsiders, Backward Glances*, Duke University Press, Durham and London, 1988.

Sung Y. W. & Lee M. K., *The Other Hong Kong Report 1991*, The Chinese University Press, Hong Kong, 1991.

Sutton, P. (ed.), *Dreamings: The Art of Aboriginal Australia*, Viking Penguin, Victoria, 1989.

Szeto, N. Y. Y. & Garrett, V. M., *Children of the Gods, Dress and Symbolism in China*, Urban Council, Hong Kong, 1990.

Szuman, S., *Dawne kilimy w Polsce i na Ukrainie [Ancient Kilims in Poland and in Ukraine]*, Poznañ, 1929 (abstract in French).

Taylor, J., *Tools of the Trade: The Art and Craft of Carpentry*, Chronicle Books, San Francisco, 1996.

Taylor, P. M. (ed.), *Fragile Traditions: Indonesian Art in Jeopardy*, University of Hawaii Press, Honolulu, 1994.

Thackara, J. (ed.), *Design After Modernism: Beyond the Object*, Thames and Hudson, London, 1988.

Thomas, J., *Time, Culture and Identity: An Interpretive Archaeology*, Routledge, London and New York, 1996.

Thomas, N. and Losche, D. (eds), *Double Vision: Art Histories and Colonial Histories in the Pacific*, Cambridge University Press, Cambridge, New York and Melbourne, 1999.

Thompson, B. (ed.), *Forceps of Language*, Craft Realities, University of Technology, Sydney, 1992.

Timms, E. and Collier, P. (eds), *Visions and Blueprints: Avant-Garde Culture and Radical Politics in*

Early Twentieth-Century Europe, Manchester University Press, Manchester, 1988.

Todd, I., 'Excavations at Sanida', *RDAC* 1992, 75–193. Notes p.14, 19, 20, 21.

Turner, V., *The Ritual Process. Structure and Anti-Structure*, Aldine Publishing Company, Chicago, 1969.

Vogel, S. (ed.), *Africa Explores: 20th Century African Art*, Centre for African Art, New York and Prestel, Munich, 1993.

Weiner, A., *Inalienable Possessions: The Paradox of Keeping While Giving*, University of California Press, Berkeley, 1992.

Wild, J. P., *Textiles in Archaeology*, Shire Publications, Aylesbury UK, 1988.

Williams, R., *The Politics of Modernism: Against the New Conformists* (ed. Pinkney, T.), Verso, London and New York, 1989.

Wood Conroy, D., 'Curating textiles: tradition as transgression', *Object*, no. 4, 1994–95, pp.19–23.

Wood Conroy, D., 'Solving Baas Becking: a sense of infinite order', *Object*, no. 3, 1994, pp.28–31.

Wood Conroy, D., *Texts from the Edge; Tapestry and Identity in Australia*, ex. cat., Jam Factory, Adelaide, 1994–1995, pp. 1–5; reprinted in *Periphery*, no. 22, February 1995, pp. 11–15.

Woodham, J. M., *Twentieth Century Design*, Oxford University Press, Oxford, 1997.

Yves Abrious, *Ian Hamilton Finlay: A visual primer*, The MIT Press, Cambridge, Mass. 1992.

GLOSSARY

ajrakh	a resist block-printed cloth, printed on both sides. Usually in blue (indigo), red and black using geometric patterns. (Kutch, Sind and Rajasthan)
bagh	meaning, garden. Name given to a type of phulkari.
dharma	religious duty, by extension socio-cosmic moral order in its entirety (Hindu)
durree	a kind of cotton carpet, usually rectangular (India)
gelim	plain woven carpet without knots
huaniu	the buttons and loops made by hand to fasten the *qi pao* or *cheung sam* at the collar and upper bodice. They performed both a functional and decorative role, and some were highly ornate and known as 'flower buttons'
ikat	woven fabric in which the pattern is tie-dyed in the threads before weaving
inma	traditional Pitjanjatjara ceremonial dancing
jala	hand-woven brocade work, similar in appearance to Jacqurard weaving
jap	see *zikr*
khadi	hands-spun and hand-woven cotton cloth
khanum	rhythmical sound
Kobhar ghar	marital room, or space
kurta	knee-length collarless shirt/tunic with sleeves, worn by men
mandarin squares	another term for the embroidered squares depicting various birds and animals attached to the front and back of the robes of Chinese court officials to denote their rank during theMing (1368–1644) and Qing (1644–1911) dynasties
milpatjunanyi	traditional Pitjanjatjara story-telling accompanied by the drawing of designs in sand

naksha	harness to lift wrap to aid in weaving *jala*
phulkari	'flowering work'. Head-covers and garments embroidered by women in northern India, mainly in the Punjab
qanat	panel of a tent
qi pao	literally, a 'banner' gown in Mandarin Chinese, refers to the close-fitting side-fastening woman's dress with a high collar and slits at the hem worn during the twentieth century by Chinese women. It is particularly associated with Hong Kong, where it was called by its Cantonese name, *cheung sam* or *cheongsam*
Quran bag	an envelope-shaped bag to keep the Quran in
sari	seamless length of cloth (5–6 metres) which forms the main part of an Indian Lady's dress
shalwar kameez	outfit of loose trousers (*shalwar*) worn with *kameez*, a long tunic. Worn mostly by women, especially in North India and Pakistan
shamiana	fabric canopy or tent used at large public gatherings
sujani	type of quilting normally used for bedcovers (Bihar)
tjanting	metal vessel with closed spout from which hot wax trickles onto cloth to create batik designs
tjap	metal (copper) stamp with which fabric is printed with hot wax during the batik process to form repeat designs
zikr	a prayer, incantation

TEXTILE ART BOOKS FROM TELOS

Art Textiles of the World

Lavishly illustrated profiles of leading textile artists from around the world.

Art Textiles of the World: Australia
Edited by Matthew Koumis with an essay by Sue Rowley
Featuring Patricia Black, Elena Gallegos, Pam Gaunt, Ruth Hadlow, Jan Irvine-Nealie, Elsje van Keppel (King), Valerie Kirk, Tori de Mestre, Patrick Snelling, Utopia Awely Batik Aboriginal Corporation
• 96pp • 52 col. illus. • 286 x 242mm
• ISBN 1 902015 70 5 • softback only • £25 €39,50 $45

Art Textiles of the World: Great Britain vol 1
Edited with an introduction by Matthew Koumis with an essay by Amanda Fielding
Featuring Dawn Dupree, Sara Brennan, Sally Greaves-Lord, Nicola Henley, Marta Rogoyska, Lynn Setterington, Jo Barker, Greg Parsons, Jeanette Appleton, Kate Blee
• 112pp • 105 col. Illus • 286 x 242mm
• ISBN 1 902015 72 1 • softback only • £25 €39,50 $45

Art Textiles of the World: Great Britain vol 2
Edited with an introduction by Jennifer Harris
Featuring Janet Ledsham, Michael Brennand-Wood, Jo Budd, Caroline Broadhead, Shelly Goldsmith, Rushton Aust, Lesley Mitchison, Polly Binns, Sally Freshwater, Alice Kettle
• 96pp • 52 col. illus. • 286 x 242mm
• ISBN 1 902015 76 4 • softback only • £25 €39,50 $45

Art Textiles of the World: Japan vol 1
Edited with an introduction by Matthew Koumis and an essay by Keiko Kawashima
Featuring Shindo Hiroyuki, Takada Yuko, Tanaka Chiyoko, Honda Masashi, Kobayashi Masakazu, Kobayashi Naomi, Honma Haruko, Agano Machiko, Shimada Kiyonori, Uemae Chiyu, Toyazaki Mitsuo, Fujino Yasuko, Bamba Masae
• 128pp • 116 col. illus, 14 b&w illus. • 286 x 242mm
• ISBN 1 902015 74 8 • softback only • £25 €39,50 $45

Art Textiles of the World: Japan vol 2
Edited by Matthew Koumis with an introduction by Keiko Kawashima and Laurel Reuter
Featuring Tetsuo Fujimoto, Shihoko Fukumoto, Yuka Kawai, Kyoko Kumai, Jun Mitsuhashi, Noriko Narahira, Suzumi Noda, Chika Ohgi, Hiroko Ohte, Takehiko Sanada, Hisako Sekijima, Reiko Sudo, Koji Takaki, Tsuguo Yanai
• 96pp • 90 col. illus., 10 b&w illus. • 286 x 242mm
• ISBN 1 902015 02 9 • softback only • £25 €39,50 $45

Art Textiles of the World: USA vol 1
Edited with an introduction by Matthew Koumis and an essay by Ilze Aviks
Featuring Kyoung Ae Cho, Virginia Davis, Deborah Fisher, Ann Hamilton, Linda Hutchins, Jane Lackey, Susan Lordi Marker, Charlene Nemec-Kessel, Jason Pollen, Jane Sauer
• 94pp • 61 col. illus., 10 b&w illus. • 286 x 242mm
• ISBN 1 902015 71 3 • softback only • £25 €39,50 $45

Art Textiles of the World: The Netherlands
Edited with an introduction by Dery Timmer and an essay by Ietse Meij
Featuring Marijke Arp, Sonja Besselink, Marian Bijlenga, Hil Driessen, Maryan Geluk, Ella Koopman, Wilma Kuil, Nel Linssen, Karola Pezarro, Marian Smit
• 96pp • 52 col. illus., 10 b&w illus. • 286 x 242mm
• ISBN 1 902015 06 1 • softback only • £25 €39,50 $45

Art Textiles of the World: Scandinavia vol 1
Edited with an introduction by Matthew Koumis
Featuring Ane Henriksen, Astrid Krogh (Denmark); Aino Kajaniemi, Piila Saksela, Ulla-Maija Vikman (Finland); Hildur Bjarnadottir, Anna Lindal (Iceland); Gunvor Nervold Antonsen, Inger-Johanne Brautaset, Marianne Mannsaker, Wagle & Lovaas(Norway); Annika Ekdahl (Sweden)
• 112pp • 100 col. illus. 14 b&w illus. • 286 x 242mm
• ISBN 1 902015 01 0 • softback only • £25 €39,50 $45

Reinventing Textiles

Reinventing Textiles Vol 2: Gender & Identity
Edited with an introduction by Professor Janis Jefferies
Essays by Sarat Maharaj (UK); Renée Baert (Canada); Giorgia Volpe & Mariette Bouillet (Canada); Alison Ferris (USA); Peter Hobbs (Canada); Kay Lawrence (Australia) & Lindsay Obermeyer (USA); Barbara Layne (Canada); Greg Kwok Keung Leong (Australia); Victoria Lynn (Australia); Tina Sherwell (Israel); Sun Jung Kim (Korea); and Lisbeth Tolstrup (Denmark)
• 168pp • 17 col. illus., 24 b&w illus. • 230 x 160mm
• ISBN 1 902015 10 X • softback only • £19.50 €29,25 $35

Reinventing Textiles Vol 3: Postcolonialism and Creativity
Edited with an introduction by Paul Sharrad & Anne Collett
Essays by Jill Baird, Vivian Campbell, Anne Collett, Diana Wood Conroy, Jasleen Dhamija, Janis Jefferies, Ruth Hadlow, Jessica Hemmings, Marianne Hulsboch, Kay Lawrence, Sharon Peoples, Paul Sharrad, Gail Tremblay
•192pp • 16 col. illus., 19 b&w illus. • 230 x 160mm
• ISBN 1 902015 12 6 • softback only • £19.50 €29,25 $35

Order your specialist textile books online at www.arttextiles.com

Portfolio Collection

Each volume:
• 28 col illus. • 48pp • softback only • 220 x 220mm • £12.50 €18,95 $19.95

Vol 1: **Jilly Edwards** by Lene Bragger
• ISBN 1 902015 20 7

Vol 2: **Marian Bijlenga** by G. Staal
• ISBN 1 902015 21 5

Vol 3: **Caroline Broadhead** by J. Theophilus
• ISBN 1 902015 23 1

Vol 4: **Chika Ohgi** by K. Kawashima
• ISBN 1 902015 25 8

Vol 5: **Anne Marie Power** by Dr J. Peers
• ISBN 1 902015 26 6

Vol 6: **Anne Wilson** by T. Porges & H. Gordon
• ISBN 1 902015 22 3

Vol 8: **Helen Lancaster** by C. Skinner
• ISBN 1 902015 29 0

Vol 9: **Kay Lawrence** by Dr D. Wood Conroy
• ISBN 1 902015 28 2

Vol 10: **Joan Livingstone** by Gerry Craig
• ISBN 1 902015 27 4

Vol 11: **Marian Smit** by M. v. der Stoep
• ISBN 1 902015 32 0

Vol 12: **Tanaka Chiyoko** by Lesley Millar
• ISBN 1 902015 24 X

Vol 14: **Lia Cook** by Jenni Sorkin
• ISBN 1 902015 34 7

Vol 15: **Jane Lackey** by Helga Pakasaar
• ISBN 1 902015 35 5

Vol 16: **Gerhardt Knodel** by Marsha Miro
• ISBN 1 902015 47 9

Vol 17: **Kyoung Ae Cho** by H. L. Hix
• ISBN 1 902015 35 5

Vol 18: **Jason Pollen** by H. L. Hix
• ISBN 1 902015 73 8

Vol 19: **Barbara Layne** by Cheryl Simon
• ISBN 1 902015 75 4

Vol 20: **Kay Sekimachi** by Yoshiko Wada
• ISBN 1 902015 77 0

Vol 21: **Emily DuBois** by Melissa Leventon
• ISBN 1 902015 38 X

Vol 22: **Gyöngy Laky** by Janet Koplos
• ISBN 1 902015 39 8

Vol 23: **Virginia Davis** by Laurel Reuter
• ISBN 1 902015 40 1

Vol 24: **Piper Shepard** by William Easton
• ISBN 1 902015 81 9

Vol 25: **Valerie Kirk** by Anne Brennan
• ISBN 1 902015 37 1

Vol 26: **Annet Couwenberg** by Auther & Lerner
• ISBN 1 902015 79 7

Vol 27: **Susan Lordi Marker** by Hildreth York
• ISBN 1 902015 41 X

Vol 28: **Agano Machiko** by Laurel Reuter
• ISBN 1 902015 59 2

Vol 29: **Fukumoto Shihoko** by U. Takeo
• ISBN 1 902015 61 4

Vol 30: **Cynthia Schira** by Joan Simon
• ISBN 1 902015 63 0

Vol 31: **Kumai Kyoko** by Ryoko Kuroda
• ISBN 1 902015 65 7

Vol 32: **Susie Brandt** by J. Courtney & S. Sachs
• ISBN 1 902015 67 3

Vol 33: **Darrel Morris** by A. Ferris & A. Wiens
• ISBN 1 902015 69 X

Vol 34: **Pauline Burbidge** by J. Duffey Harding
• ISBN 1 902015 71 1

Vol 35: **Norma Minkowitz** by K. Whitney
• ISBN 1 902015 91 6

Vol 36: **Merle Temkin** by Lois Martin
• ISBN 1 902015 92 4

Vol 37: **Joan Truckenbrod** by Polly Ullrich
• ISBN 1 902015 93 2

Vol 38: **Norma Starszakowna**
• ISBN 1 902015 95 9